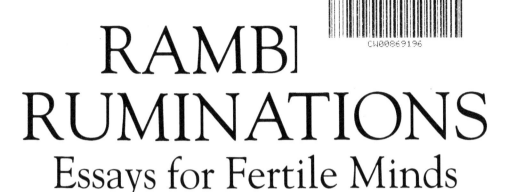

RAMBI
RUMINATIONS
Essays for Fertile Minds

R. KERMIT HILL, JR.

outskirts
press

Introduction

I began writing these essays in 2005 to let off steam and to retain my thoughts. I don't have a great memory. My little ego seems to want to pass these thoughts on. One of my terrifying traits as a teacher was that I wanted to make people think, to ask, "Why?" I retired in 2008, but the bug is still with me. There appears to be no antivirus.

I learned a lot from my students over time. These essays are a mental chewing-on-life. I hope they are homogenized, grade A and stinkweed free. When my typewriter ribbons went up four times in price, I dragged myself into the modern age, kicking and screaming, I suppose. Anyway, I have a computer full of these ruminations. About half of them have been published in the *Weed Hitching Post* monthly newsletter in the southern wilds of New Mexico on the edge of the earth. If places referred to puzzle you, I suggest a good atlas or two for your library, and, of course, you can google them. The first 22 essays and the last herein were published in the *Hitching Post* from 2017 to 2020.

I must thank my wonderful wife of 50 years, Wendy, for all she has done to help me.

TABLE OF CONTENTS

ON THE FLAG

I WAS FOR some reason reminded today about the unit I used to do with 8th graders on the flag and patriotism. Their assignment was to create a flag representing themselves based on symbols and color psychology. I started this unit because of all the hullabaloo about patriotism in the 1960-70 period when people were burning flags over Vietnam and civil rights.

The unit included a history of our flag and comments on others—especially the Confederacy, Texas and the Germans. Ain't it interesting that those dingbats in the south have been so super patriotic of late when they wanted to break up the nation in 1861. Well, we humans are interesting critters, aren't we? I am reminded that Lincoln refused to take the southern states' stars off the flag, referring to them as our erring sisters.

The unit also examined the history of patriotic thought in the U.S. and what it is we swear our allegiance to. That was another issue—the mandating of saying the Pledge of Allegiance in schools daily, a practice I fully disagree with. Why? Because it deflates the meaning of it all, and kids don't even know what they are saying half the time. It is brainwashing of the worst sort. Too many people don't bother to note the last phrase, "with liberty and justice for all."

So, we come to the greatest moment in the story of the flag. Now the flag is a symbol, not a holy relic. Keep that in mind. What would you judge to be that moment? I'd place my bet on most people remembering the Iwo Jima scene. Here is my vote.

It is 1936. Hitler is in power and already persecuting various people. The Olympics have been assigned to Berlin. For all our own faults, the U.S. team has a contingent of Black men who will create a legend. I have stood in that stadium looking at their names on a wall and felt shivers in my spine. The teams enter in the opening parade and each team lowers its flag, perhaps even waves it before Hitler. Many face him with fascist-style salutes, which he returns. The United States comes last. They march, not slouch. They tip their straw hats to him, and the flag does not dip—it stands upright. Hitler is doomed. We do not dip our flag to anyone—not king, nor tyrant nor pope—not even our own president, for it is the flag of the American people, who kiss no man's hand or butt. Those who wrap themselves in the flag and those who burn it are equally wrong—perhaps evil is not too strong a term. The flag belongs up there on the pole, above us all. It belongs to no group, no god nor individual, but represents us all.

That moment in Berlin should be taught to every child in this country at the same time as the last line of the Pledge. That is the greatest moment in the history of the flag.

ON LOVE

In 25 words or less, define *love*. I love my wife of almost 50 years. She is beautiful, kind, smart, sweet, caring, fun and sexy. I knew I loved her immediately, proposed after two weeks and the rest is history. I love my children. It is difficult to explain that love—it just is, perhaps because it involved an act of creation. They are great kids, and I am proud of them—not because they are perfect—just because they are. I guess it is the same with my grandchildren, only they are more miraculous, if that is possible. I had reached a state where I thought I would never have grandchildren—and bingo!

I love my parents, brother, aunts and uncles. Many of them are gone, but I still love their memories. They all have helped define my life. I love my friends and acquaintances because they, too, are good people who give me definition. I think the word *loyalty* comes into play here. I go to former coworkers' funerals out of loyalty.

Old girlfriends—of course. One should never say, "I love you," to someone if you intend to retract it. Love should be forever; otherwise, it's just sex. However, old girlfriends also can cause a lot of pain. I have loved a string of dogs, which seems to work about as well as loving people.

I love New Mexico for its people, its landscape and its climate, yet I can feel little things for faraway Scotland. It is hard to love a large country, parts of which I have never seen, but I do love it. That is not to say I dislike the rest of the world, but it is very hard to love all of mankind or a planet.

Still, I love the heavens, the universe and nature. I love food and music, the seasons, literature, drama and paintings. I love history, humor and home. I love flowers, trees, wild animals, the sea, mountains, snow and rain. I must conclude that I cannot define love in 25 words or less. Sorry, Love.

Humans are selfish by nature. They look after their self-interests. This is not inherent evil—it is about survival, which is instinctual. If humans are selfish, blame God. Selfishness is a major factor in defining love. Selfishness is often confused with love. It has been oft stated that sacrifice is the truest expression of love. Remember God and Abraham, long before God and Jesus. We give up things—time, money, energy, our own selfish needs—to help others. It has been said that one of the deepest forms of love is that of the soldier for his fellow soldier. The ultimate sacrifice of life is emblematic of the deepest love of tribe, family or country.

A modern twist on this theme is the sacrifice of caregivers for the ill or elderly, and it is pointing to the fact that sacrifice overdone detracts from survival, just as too many dead young men on the battlefield detract from the gene pool. Too much time, energy and money spent on others may grind down the caregiver, whether it is parent or child.

Our definition of *love* is always in the end caught up in selfishness—we expect some reward, some warmth or recognition, some reason to go on. We are ultimately nearly always confused about these issues. Without love, we are incomplete, seeking and hurting.

Sacrifice without reward is guaranteed to produce bitterness. Sacrifice repaid with abuse will arouse anger. Our selfish side must have a positive response, and why not? To welcome abuse in payment for sacrifice, to play the martyr simply isn't healthy, try as we may to convince ourselves that the keys to heaven lie in accepting that abuse. Abuse begets abuse.

Even Mother Teresa got her rewards. You can be certain that it pleased her to be doing what she did and pleased her more when it drew attention to the plight of her people. I am not being cynical when I report this—I am just looking at the world as it is with a great deal of eternal hope. Perhaps love does make the world go round.

One of the great euphemisms of all time is *making love—sleeping together* is another. No wonder we are a collective psychological mess. We can't distinguish sex, sleep and love. Love is a many splintered thing.

ON TRIBALISM

WE ARE TRIBAL critters, and we do not change tribes easily. This is due to internal and external pressures. Internally, we just don't want to give up our close relationships. Externally, prejudices retard our assimilation—prejudices from both other tribes and our own.

Survival on this planet is a tough proposition. Tribes have always competed for limited resources and have concerned themselves with reproduction aimed at increasing their numbers. These are emotional issues; reason is too often not involved. Hence, humans overdo it: overbreed, overuse, go over there looking for resources, including women, which other tribes already claim.

What makes one group more aggressive than another is debated with great emotion. Is it because they think they are God's chosen people? Is it genetics, culture, climate or topography? Or is it most of the above?

This brings me to two tribes close to New Mexico hearts—the Japanese and the New Mexico National Guard 200th Coast Artillery. Both would suffer immensely from the collision. What traits did they have in common? Both were poor, both were populated by exotic peoples (in the eyes of dominant Northwestern European culture), and both bred a warrior class. Both would see the first three atomic bombs explode.

I want to focus here on the first point. As the world industrialized and science allowed for the rapid growth of populations, Japan worked to become a modern, self-sufficient nation, much as people in New Mexico dreamed the same dreams. However, I fear that in both places lack of resources hindered them and thereby engendered psychological feelings of inferiority and jealous anger.

The period from the American Civil War through World War II encompasses the great world imperialization, and it was accompanied by tremendous prejudices based on racial, ethnic, religious and economic differences which were approached with ignorance, nationalism, arrogance and fear. Rarely did anyone look carefully at geographic causes or scientific reasons as explanations for differences or similarities. Even anthropology was perverted in service to tribal bigotry.

So, the atrocities of the 20th and 21st centuries progressed. They were not new in shape but have been made much larger by technology. Tribalism has not diminished. Rather, it is an element of human sickness. What are we to do about that ailment? It would be nice if we could overcome fear. Perhaps it is simply too deeply bred into us to need a tribal identity, which rests in large part on fear of the other combined with a sense of identity. Further, it gives us assurance that we are worth something.

I write this on Super Bowl Sunday, February 2, 2014, as we await the issue. Shall our own great Mile High Denver Broncos be victorious, our magic orange-and-blue reign supreme? Or shall the forces of darkness, of the wet, cold, sea-girded Hawks prevail? And, if they do, what have we done wrong to deserve such outrageous fortune? Need I say more? But wait—another problem has arisen. Our neighboring Broncos have tried to steal our green chile: elixir of our lives, our claim to culinary and horticultural fame, our sacred vegetable. Oh, horror upon horror! What hath our clan done to deserve this gross miscarriage of tribal loyalty? Does this mean WAR?

On Art

I MAY NOT know much about art, but I know what I like. Anyone wishing to drive art, or art history teachers, crazy should say this to them. Each of us knows what we want on the walls of our home or workplace, and no arrogant snob of an art dogmatist has any right to tell us otherwise, because he isn't in our head.

Why do we like art, and how should we judge it? Fine art is the product of professionals who spend their time and effort perfecting their craft. Each of them has his or her creative genius, ability or vision. Some are technically proficient without great creativity. Others may see new visions of truth but not become as proficient with the tools of their art form.

We like color, nature, drama, sound, form and texture. These give life meaning, make it worthwhile. This is just the way we are. Ultimately, what is good is a matter of democracy: the piece that receives the most visitors, the longest gazes, and the most perceptive comments is the better piece, no matter what Mr. Art Fascist says. This may take centuries, however. Tastes change, individually and collectively. Beauty is in the eye of the beholder.

Why are we not all artists? Well, in one way we are. We just aren't professionals, nor can we be. We do have artistic impulses. They may be expressed by collecting or criticizing or by spectating as much as by doing. The painter or writer or musician without an audience is doomed economically.

Wide dissemination and appreciation of the arts runs up against obstacles. Lack of money is one. Lack of education and ignorance is another. Perhaps there are psychological obstacles, too, though they are fewer. The number of blind or deaf people is relatively small. Religious and philosophical objections to art appear throughout history. Feeding the body comes before worrying about the soul, so money, time and energy spent on art seem sinfully wasteful to some. Stimulation of the senses is objectionable to others. "Thou shalt not worship idols," say yet others.

Art is clearly woven tightly into our spiritual needs. Much of what we decorate with constitutes our household gods, and these objects are far more pervasive than we realize. I think one who truly worshipped no idols would be a dreadfully lifeless, gray, harsh being—exactly the way we portray ascetic fanatics of the most dangerous type. A man with bad art around him is better than one with no art. A man who cannot see beauty and thinks others should not see it either is truly a lost soul.

On Fear

"All we have to fear is fear itself,
fear which paralyzes needed effort."
FDR, March 1933
The most cogent, intelligent, rational statement ever made by a leader.

So, CLASS, LET us make a list of our fears, that we might better understand our paralysis.

We are afraid of Nature, the dark, the sun, ETs, death, life, disease, guns, terrorists, homos, sex, no sex, starving, fat, chemicals, nukes, kooks, eco-nazis, eco-nuts, foreigners, immigrants, Moslems, Christians, Jews, Hindus, Buddhists, atheists, lack of oil, oil spills, fracking, drought, floods, storms, El Nino, lack of jobs, economic failure, egomania, weak egos, tribalism, disappearance of tribal existence, snakes, spiders, bats, bears, wildcats, A bombs, sharks, criminals, policemen, drugs, pain, drug pushers (pharmaceutical companies included), mice, rats, plague, ebola, flu, Zitas, zits, freezing, starving, fire, liberals, conservatives, nazis, commies, anarchists, democrats, republicans, kings, dictators, popes, fanatics, ideas, modernism, nightmares, drunk drivers, isolation, crowds, low testosterone, low estrogen, old age, baldness, prematurely gray hair, saggy boobs, flab, tobacco, pot, additives, the boss, the teacher, the students, fellow workers, jealous mates, jealous lovers, our parents, our kids, freaks, weirdos, gun nuts, heights, claustrophobia, the ocean, the desert, the woods, wolves, witches, ghosts, demons, the devil, ogres, evil dwarfs, chemicals, BO, dogs, cats, time, dirt, machines, technology, flying monkeys, dragons, meteors, tsunamis, earthquakes, tornadoes, typhoons, Godzilla, Leviathan, pirates, mobsters, sirens, seductresses, betrayal, neediness in extremis, losing seasons, bad omens, lawyers, doctors, witch doctors, politicians, primitive people, nomads, the rich, the poor, neurosis, psychosis, halitosis, a bad prognosis, eternal damnation, eternal nothingness, success, failure, slavery, unions, the vastness of the universe, ignorance, intelligence, strange sounds, strange smells, strange people, strange skies, chaos, falling, flying, water, drowning, thirst, bugs, spooks, spirits, spies, looking foolish, looking weak, being ugly, radio waves, rejection, bullies, zombies, non-existence, loss of power, being lost, making mistakes, ridicule, poverty, the unknown, war, boredom, the enemy gods, psychos, climate change, the future, the past, vampires, yetis, Lloronas, sasquatches, Doña Sebastiana, giants, volcanoes, the sun not returning north, moon lunacy, gangs, other tribes, other races, black, red, lilac, bankruptcy, foreclosure, stock market crashes, acne, bad breath, needle shots, bad dreams, loss of memory, getting lost, responsibility, cowardice, being tongue-tied, getting caught, lice, fleas, mosquitoes, not being asked to the prom, ED, blindness, deafness, inability to dance, and our own shadow. I am sure each of you can add one more item to vastly increase the list.

And we wonder why we can't sleep well or get things done, why we need drugs. The true miracle of our existence is that we function at all. I fear no one is listening.

On July 4ᵗʜ, the Royals, and Civil War

A friend in our book group, a native of Massachusetts, says the events of 1775-1783 were a civil war, not a revolution. This gives one cause for thought. The issue was perhaps just a matter of equal representation, and had Jolly Old England given in on *Rule Britannia*, we might still be loyal members of the Empire. One thing makes me wonder if we, in fact, are. Personally, as a geography and history person and a believer in manifest destiny, I am prone to opt for the revolution motif.

The bothersome matter alluded to above is that every time I scan the news online or walk past a magazine rack in the store, I am left wondering how it is that we are so ruled by Kate and William and Harry and Meghan and Andrew and Liz and her corgis and Philip and Charles and the ghost of Diana and on and on. What in the name of Washington, Jefferson, Adams and Franklin is going on here?

Okay. We speak the same language, more or less, kinda sorta. We fly the same colors, have some of the same music and religion, similar political theories and quite a few of the same surnames and place names. We even retain some culinary similarities, though chile helps a lot. Still, I wonder. So, I must tell you a story.

In 1985, my brother-in-law was awarded a sabbatical to Oxford, and the family immediately invited us over. The kids were 10 and 7, and we were poor, but we got an unexpected gift from someone with Weed connections, so we decided to go for three weeks. Unfortunately, Weed then decided to celebrate its 100-year anniversary that June, and we missed *Little Joe the Wrangler.*

Instead, we helped the Queen celebrate her birthday in London. We actually have celebrated the 4th in England—in 1970, while in Coventry, where our independence was recognized.

The parade was quite a spectacle, and we stood right on the front row, watching the whole royal family, Diana included, go by—twice! There were lots of red coats and bands and jets overhead. *Hail Britannia!* Well, we did our part to maintain good relations and show no hard feelings about Bunker Hill or the burning of D.C. or the Alabama claims, even if, red-blooded American boy that I am, I find all that royal stuff to be nonsense. But it is entertaining in some strange way. We also paid our respects to Shakespeare, Nessy, Dad's old Army Air Force bases, Yorkshire and Glasgow—where the Hill family came from—and met two of our daughter's pen pals.

There was a long-term result of the trip, too. We planted the travel bug in our kids. Our daughter went to Franklin and Marshall and married a grad of William and Mary—go figure. In the Foreign Service and even before, she has seen a lot of the planet. Our son has seen his share, too. Both spent their junior year of college in Germany. And let us remember that a lot of the world has come here, often as not, to escape the bad behavior of kings and other despots. My wife is of Norwegian, French and Rhineland ancestry. Oh, yes, we were immigrants.

Children need to be independent and should become different people than their parents, otherwise we would still be oysters, and that is not what the Creator intended nor destined. I wonder, too, if the current royals are just a product of Hollywood and Madison Avenue. Anyway, on the 4th let us raise a salute to Old Glory and be thankful that we are an independent people dedicated to equality for all. It appears that maybe the Brits have learned something from us. Parents do sometimes learn from their children.

On Motor Vehicles

Back in April, I gave a paper at the Historical Society convention in Alamogordo about a Mescalero Indian agent—at least, that is what it started off to be, but I got diverted onto a side road and, as often happens, one road leads to another. A few ruminations back, I included a graph which demonstrated how the rate of change has soared upward in the last 150 years. In the middle of my research, it hit me that the agent was faced with a serious uphill struggle. He was trying to help a people barely out of the Stone Age to enter the age of automobiles, airplanes, electricity, movies and so on. Then I remembered Geronimo's Cadillac, and I picked up a story about the Osage tribe in Oklahoma who, in 1911, owned more autos than any other comparably sized group in the world. Why? Because they lived on top of an oil field.

Well, my feeble old brain slowly ground into a higher gear (I didn't get a driver's license until I was out of high school). I wondered if, of all the inventions in the last two centuries, the internal combustion engine has had the greatest impact on the world. We do love our wheels, whatever form they come in. That includes books, TV and movies— *The Dukes of Hazzard*, for instance. The auto-racing business made one New Mexico family, the Unsers, famous. My mother's younger brother was a mechanical genius and owned a very good dirt-track racer. Tony Hillerman's Navajo mysteries are totally dependent on police cars.

We love them so much that we are blind to any negative effects they have on us. This is, in some ways, quite understandable. I can only stay attached to Sacramento by car. Automobiles have opened up the world to me through travel. How boring life would be if I couldn't go into town a couple of times a day. We gain a sense of freedom, power and attractiveness, in some cases, from our wheels. My father's family was poor, and they did not own cars. He bought his first after World War II, used. He was very proud of the '54 Buick he bought while at Weed. It was a status symbol—he had arrived. Mom's family had several cars and her mother drove—feminism on wheels.

In the next two months I took another side road, which may have been triggered by hearing that automobiles have caused more American deaths and injuries than all our wars combined. The same is even more true regarding drug deaths. Consider, too, that one drug—alcohol—combined with cars has been especially deadly. Humans don't always deal well with statistics.

Virtually every war fought since 1900 has involved control of oil and gas. When the Germans in World War II were retreating using horses, the U.S. Army was fully supplied by trucks driven, by the way, mostly by Black soldiers. By the 1950s, air pollution—smog—was choking many places. We got a good dose of that in the year we spent in California in the mid-50s. While that issue has been addressed, it is not over with. We must wonder what toll has been taken by long commutes, traffic jams and so on. Road rage is one name for it. Insurance laws hurt, too. I don't think you had to insure your horse at Weed in 1900.

Finally, let us note the impact on our country when we began to slip as a world leader in auto production. The fault lay in our own ownership, management and labor. In 1970, when Chevrolet took advantage of the American people via the unions sabotaging cars and management refusing to adopt production checks, we went abroad. To Japan. If they ever want to apologize, I might consider returning to Chevy. In the meantime, the impact on the American working class has not been pretty.

We love our vehicles, though, don't we? August has always been a good month for road trips. Maybe we'll see you somewhere on the road—that has a faint sound of a song—and, if not, we'll definitely come home to the Agua Chiquita.

ON AN ODYSSEY TO OZ

IN MID-AUGUST, WE went east to visit our daughter in Maryland/D.C. We needed a rest and there was too much to see, so we took it somewhat easy. Being away from home helped. However, one is quickly overwhelmed there by a variety of features. This was not our first visit. I think I've been there 10 times. If you have never been, be prepared for a shock. If you have, be glad you are here. Off we go.

It took us 6½ hours to reach Baltimore from our door in Santa Fe. The flight is roughly 3½ hours. Once there, it can take an hour to go 8-10 miles in the city. D.C. itself is 68.34 square miles, the greater D.C. area about double that, and Otero County is 6,628 square miles with 63,797 people; D.C. has 3 million. I leave the rest of that math to you. New Mexico is 121,590 square miles and has 2 million people. Traffic lights are multitudinous, as is traffic, so travel is generally slow by car and no better by bus. Subways give some relief.

Vegetation is jungle-like and very green. One can rarely see any distance, even though the landscape is not flat for the most part. Trees are mostly deciduous and often quite large. In fact, there is a little-known logging business in the region. Steep hills are common. Where commercial city replaces woods, the buildings cut off nearly all views of the distance. Being used to seeing Mount Taylor 90 miles from my house, this is disturbing. It is compounded by the climate. The heat and humidity of summer nearly knocks you back in the door when you step out. One sweats a lot there.

The use of electricity is ginormous, so there are very large power lines everywhere. We saw four in the relatively short distance from D.C to Baltimore. This makes the area livable. In the early 1800s, it wasn't. In fact, it suffered both malaria and yellow fever epidemics. Drainage, sewers and so on are important.

The importance of land and long views must have an impact on the mind and psyche. Perhaps it turns people inward. Often the skies are gray for days on end. We had one partially clear day out of six. On a little trip outward, it was a thrill just to get a glimpse of the Blue Ridge Mountains. The dearth of farming and livestock in far northern Virginia was discouraging, however. Part of the reason is the growth of the metropolitan area, which makes housing development more valuable. Those of you raising cattle in New Mexico would have been shocked by what wasn't being used.

Human diversity is major in Oz. You can probably find about any kind of human there is there, but some stand out. Having been in the slave south, African Americans abound. There is a Chinatown. Various Hispanics and Jews are apparent. In fact, I was very aware of houses of worship. The Mormons sort of go overboard. Baptist, Methodist and Presbyterian churches are plentiful. Catholics seem less so by northern New Mexico standards. Liberalism is common, but the balance was hard to judge.

We ate seafood, French food, Italian food and fairly plain old American food, including North Carolina-style pulled pork out in the country. The Italian adventure was with our lobbyist nephew and family, from whom we learned that the Comet Ping Pong pizza place had been shot up by a nutcase not long ago who thought it was being used to traffic children. There were a lot of children there that night. Parents were taking their little ones into a cool nearby bookstore, too. The nutcase shooter does not strike me as an educated person.

We had already seen most of the major attractions and the White

House didn't have time for me, so here are a few things we did enjoy. The kids took us to the Marines' Friday night parade at their barracks. That was quite impressive and tastefully done. We met a young Marine from Farmington of Pueblo Indian ancestry. It was my birthday—nice of them to play for me. We also had a brief tour of the National War College. We saw the Dumbarton Oaks mansion and gardens in Georgetown. This was the site of several Allied meetings in World War II. While there, a jetliner took off roughly once per minute from National Airport. We picked up our son-in-law at the National Defense University, where he is studying the issue of cybersecurity. Our daughter took us on a drive out past Dulles Airport, which is now surrounded by offices and tech centers, to the village of Waterford, founded in 1733 by Pennsylvania Quakers. That was the scene of some nasty guerilla warfare in the Civil War. When we crossed back into Maryland, we began to see crops—corn and soybeans—and livestock. We also sidetracked to see an aqueduct of the Baltimore and Ohio Canal crossing the Monocacy River. The aqueduct was odd enough, but I bet you never heard of the river either. It had more water than the Rio Grande. Nowadays, the canal is a bike path. We glimpsed the Capitol dome and Washington Monument once from afar.

An uncle of mine, who is buried at Arlington Cemetery, once told me I should pursue a congressional aide job and come to D.C. I said, "No, thank you. I'd rather be in Sacramento." But it takes all kinds to make a world, and someone has to keep Oz in operation.

On Ramblin'

THE HISTORY OF mankind is one of migration and mutation—change. So why is there such a fuss over some people having to move and change while we have no sympathy for others? We have all had to change. The reasons are beyond counting. Among them are climate, war, religion, politics, economics, health, drought, disease, adventure and boredom. The Indians moved from Asia. The Spanish brought horses. The Comanches loved them, much to the dismay of their neighbors, including other Indians. They lost their horses, at least for a while.

My family came to New Mexico for health reasons. My wife's family moved to Colorado for economic reasons and a new scene. The children of these families are scattered all over creation.

We suffer certain disconnects when American Indians come up, even more than we do with the African diaspora. We want to be good guys, so it is hard to face the evils of history. We are humans, and that word *human* is the key operative one. Humans are not the only thing that migrates and mutates, however. Just about everything does, including birds, bees and educated fleas.

The United States is a nation created by this process, and it is still in the process of mutating, a very natural thing. Being humans, none of us are saints, in spite of claims by a few groups. We do bemoan the fall from paradise—Eden—whatever it was. I think we romanticize the

Indians as the last people to live there. It is all a dream. I guess in each case the Edenites need to blame someone, be they Mongols, Goths, Franks, Romans, Arabs, Anglo-Saxons, Celts, Vikings, the English, and so on. Of course, we forget that the Indians imposed on each other, as did the Africans.

If the Creator wanted us to become human, then it wanted us to cease being oysters. What does it mean to be human? It means, among other things, that we change.

Change across time includes diseases—hence, devastating epidemics; the earth—hence devastating earthquakes and tsunamis; apples—hence, apple pie; and music—hence, jazz, bluegrass, C&W and so on. And had people not migrated, there would be a lot of famous people who never existed. In fact, you and I may never have existed. I don't mean to cause headaches by being so philosophical, but the teacher in me (blame it on my parents) requires that my readers think.

On a gentler note, I recognize that we all suffer a sense of loss—the loss of Eden—whether it was Scotland, Norway, Israel, Russia, Mongolia or Senegal. That sense may involve our having to deal with our world, which seems more constricted to us than we assume that old world was. I remember being in Scotland once and feeling a strong sense of *déjà vu*, a kind of sadness, but we are called on to leave behind the things of childhood, however painful the leaving is, so let us move on.

ON "AMAZING GRACE"

I AM SURPRISED that I have not written about this hymn before now, considering how much I like it. I am picky about hymns because too many are poor in melodic quality or in their message. I had not given much thought to its meanings. It has been around since the U.S. was born, and many Protestant denominations sang it, yet it did not become visibly popular until the second half of the 20th century. In the 1700s, the bagpipes were banned in the British kingdom, so when Scots and Scots-Irishmen came to America, they substituted the fiddle and other strings for the pipes and created country western music.

When JFK was assassinated in 1963, an Irish army pipe band played at his funeral. It touched something inside many of us. Glen Campbell (a Scottish name), who had New Mexico connections, learned to play the pipes and others followed. "Amazing Grace" soon became a favorite piece. The pipes began to be played at funerals, especially of policemen and firemen who were of Irish descent, and as we lost our way, mired in Vietnam, the song began to appeal to veterans. Soon, every ethnic/racial group in the country was performing it. I created a school lesson about American diversity, playing 10 versions of it and requiring students to write an essay about how it illustrated that diversity. It worked.

Why? "I once was lost, but now am found." This condition is endemic to the human species, as is often being blind to reality or the truth—we have a bad habit of seeing what we want to see. In the case of the slave trader composer John Newton, it was the evil of slavery to which he was blind until some mysterious thing opened his eyes. The second verse speaks of fear. Well, that is endemic to us, too. "All we have to fear is fear itself." Life is frightening, and we need to feel safe. We travel through life, which is filled with snares, travails, dangers and toils, and if we survive, we hope to arrive in a safe place as long as life endures, and we need all the help we can get. There is a fourth verse which indicates a timelessness about life. For we who live in an age where everything moves fast and we expect change, this is good to remember.

Whether one believes in any religion, all of them have elements of wisdom we can benefit from. There is also something very elemental about the melody, which can be played on either all black or all white keys of the piano. It may be African in origin. It is my thought that the most simple, direct melodies are what appeal to us the most. This, of course, raises questions about why music periodically becomes discordant. Life is filled with alpha and omega, and perhaps we need that to make sense of what is good and beautiful.

Here is a small list of musicians and groups who have recorded "Amazing Grace": Andean Tradition-Ecuador, Band of the Irish Guards, Scottish Borderers, Dejan's Olympia Brass-New Orleans, Chuck Mangione, Daniel Lanois-Acadie, opera soprano Jesse Norman, Willie Nelson, Charlie Rich, Canadian Brass, Hymns of Hawaii, Blind Boys of Alabama, After Class-Xylophone, Royal Scots Dragoon Guards, Welsh Guards (two versions), Atmospheres-Scottish Celtic pipes, Elvis, Randy Travis, Celtic Women, Andrea Bocelli, Alan Jackson, Aretha Franklin, Harlem Gospel Choir, Soweto Gospel Choir-African, Japanese duet on violins, Dolly Parton, Celine Dion—and I have seen three versions of it in Spanish, one of which comes from the Spanish Baptist hymnal. That's for starters. The Blind Boys of Alabama sing it to a different tune, and the Welsh Guards have a version with different words.

So, this hymn speaks to some sort of a universal human need. As Christmas approaches with its message of rebirth, let us take heed.

ON WORLD WAR I HYSTERIA

ONE HUNDRED YEARS ago, world leaders met at Versailles, France, to formally end World War I. Even though U.S. president Woodrow Wilson put forth a rational 14-point program, it was rejected, and the U.S. did not ratify the treaty. That treaty stripped Germany of power, led to Hitler, and the Americans, my father included, had to go back over there in 1943. Wilson was taken to France on the new battleship USS New Mexico, by the way. In 1916, Wilson swore we would not go to war. In 1917, he called for a declaration of war, and, in 1919, tried to create a fair treaty. The treaty that was agreed upon laid the foundation for the Vietnam War. But Americans generally rejected both Wilson and the Great War by 1920. The war to end all wars didn't. What happened?

In case you haven't noticed, humans can have strange characteristics. They are prone to *hysteria*, defined as "behavior exhibiting overwhelming or unmanageable fear and emotional excess." The stage had been set for this drama by several events and phenomena. In 1916, Pancho Villa raided Columbus, New Mexico. Widespread disease epidemics were common. A very large number of immigrants came each year—46 different languages were spoken by men who served in the U.S. military—and there was general economic insecurity. Strikes in Colorado led to the Ludlow Massacre in 1914, when the National

Guard killed a number of strikers.

New Mexico suffered its share of hysteria. The National Council of Defense clippings and letters give us examples. Most interestingly, this Council was created at the time Wilson was promising no war. Of course, he was facing re-election. Each county had a person charged with clipping war-related items from the county papers. These clippings and related letters are in the State Archives in Santa Fe.

This is my favorite: "Candy Infested with Diphtheria Germs Given to Lordsburg Tots by Man Believed to be German." The cemeteries around Weed are full of people who died of diphtheria in those days. Of course, Lordsburg is down on the Mexican border. As a side story, the Great Flu Epidemic of 1918 was spread by the war and killed far more people than the war did. Go see Ona George's grave at the Avis Cemetery. Like over half the New Mexicans in service who died, he did not even get overseas.

Elephant Butte Dam was completed in 1915. In 1917, a Las Cruces lawyer wrote, "It is our opinion that troops or other guards should be stationed at this dam." They were, and Eugene Manlove Rhodes saw a good story in it, "No Mean City," but his German bad guys fail. In 1918, Henry Wray published a magazine article titled "America's Unguarded Gateway," in which he claimed that Germany—and possibly Japan—intended to either invade the U.S. or get Mexico to via New Mexico. Mexico was neither that stupid nor organized. A group of UNM professors slammed Wray and accused him of libel.

In the fervor of war-inspired righteousness, prohibition of alcohol and women's voting rights were being advocated. Women's rights! God forbid. A Santa Fe editorial titled "Ladies and Pants" took the *Portales Journal* editor to task for attacking modern women who wore pants. Another item reads, "Governor asked to Stop Bootlegging at Albuquerque." It says bootlegging was a menace to the troops there. Women still wear pants, and prohibition failed.

The mines of the United States were very heavily dependent on immigrant labor. Headlines proclaimed, "All Coal Mines at Gallup May

Be Shut Down," followed by, "Most of the men on strike are said to be aliens, many of them Austrians." The same issues arose at Silver City and all other mining areas. The railroads, ships, electric power companies and many stoves ran on coal. No immigrants, no coal. If you ever get up to Dawson, near Raton, visit the cemetery there and check out the names of men killed in mine explosions in this period.

One thing the New Mexico papers never seemed to mention was what was happening in the Persian Gulf area. It was of great importance to all parties engaged in the war. Need three guesses as to why? Oil! However, the Las Vegas paper doesn't hesitate to tell us that "Son Is Drafted; Mother Loses Reason," with the article concluding that she was committed to the mental institution, which was a major employer in Las Vegas. I wonder if the fact that she had 14 kids had anything to do with it.

Well, the war ended, and people woke up. About 116,000 Americans died, less than half in combat, and less than half in the service went overseas.

Let us please learn a little from history.

On a Modern Plague

I STARTED THINKING about a February topic on Christmas Eve. My first idea was to find on the internet some famous people born in February. Wow! Did that set off a string of ideas!

We live in strange times, created in part by the invention of the computer and cell phones. We suffer a whole new form of addiction. The day before, we attended a performance of the Desert Chorale at St. Francis Cathedral Basilica, which is a beautiful experience. We sat among several people we know—always a heartwarming feeling. However, a young man sitting next to my wife was texting on his muted cell phone the whole time, which diminished the experience for her. Sounds disturbingly familiar, I fear. It seems some people believe the device is their brain, and the rest of the world doesn't matter.

The invention as a tool is amazing. I discovered a series of February births online, one with over 3,000 names on it. The trouble is that the vast majority of them are minor-league entertainment figures. I don't know who they are nor do I care. Of course, if I were listed, I would likely sing a different tune. Maybe this technology makes us feel good about ourselves. So, I give you a short list of names: Abraham Lincoln, George Washington, Buffalo Bill Cody, John Deere, Thomas Edison, Chuck Yeager, Robert Fulton, Charles

Darwin, Cyrus McCormick and Charles Dickens.

Two hundred years ago, you could not get a message across the Atlantic in less than a month, at best. In 1942-45, Dad was in England. His only means of communication with Mom and me was mail, telegrams and black-and-white photos sent by mail. Today, we are able to phone and skype with our daughter in Kazakhstan. She sends us color photos regularly, and she will come home this spring, by air, for a visit. We can watch a certain baby boy, wailing away, get his bath in Berkeley, almost in real time. Luckily, my wife is a cell phone/computer expert, so even this old dinosaur gets to enjoy these communications. Why, I even know how to use the contraption as an encyclopedia!

Most addictions are somehow related to pain relief. Being disconnected or far from loved ones is undoubtedly painful. However, psychologists have generally concluded that immersing oneself in the news of the day is a cause of pain because nine-tenths of it is bad news. Following it on our cell phone is not good for us.

We are also hurt when we are rejected, made to feel unpopular; hence, Facebook might seem a solution. What if you get addicted to toxic people? Going off to la-la land in the web isn't going to make us healthy in the end. It bothers me, too, when I see couples out at dinner, and both are gazing at their cell phones when they should be staring adoringly into each other's eyes and murmuring sweet words. I have alluded in past ruminations to other pains in February. It would hurt too doggone much to take an arrow in the heart. Beyond that, we have to deal with the teasing Mother Nature plays on us in February, that strange time between winter and spring. I doubt that Mother Nature has a cell phone. We just must be patient.

February is the time of Aquarius and Pisces. Aquarius is the water bearer—clouds—and Pisces is the fish. It is the last of the 12 Zodiac symbols. February is not the second month in the Roman calendar; rather, it is the last month, i.e., the end of winter. The two Zodiac signs combined are supposed to indicate people who are caring, humanitarian and have a social conscience, which translates to forgiving. February is a good time for reading books—Lincoln books, especially.

In this balancing time between winter and spring, let us work at keeping our balance.

ON TRAVELING SPUDS
AND OTHER THINGS

IN THE 1500s, a bunch of Spaniards moved to America where they discovered a new food. Spuds migrated back over the Atlantic and became known to us as the Irish potato. It was immensely popular, especially in Ireland and Germany, and it helped the population of Ireland soar to eight million in an area less than one-third the size of New Mexico. Then a bug of sorts migrated, probably from Mexico to Europe. The potato blight was a disaster, killing—mainly by starvation—around a million Irish people alone in the period 1845-1849. Two million of them migrated to the United States and others to all parts of the world. They came just as the U.S. was expanding rapidly, migrating to Oregon and New Mexico. For a brief time, spuds even migrated to the Sacramento Mountains; hence, Potato Canyon.

This expansion required cavalrymen and railway workers to do the dirty work. Guess who got the jobs. Immigrants were not appreciated then by all, just as they aren't today. A common saying in many quarters was "no Irish need apply." Much of this was fueled by religious bigotry. The wars of the Reformation were not over, it turns out. Ironically, a German immigrant named Thomas Nast loved to put down the Irish Catholics in his cartoons. He, by the way, created our Santa Claus, who is, therefore, an immigrant. By the time the next big wave came, the Irish had assimilated and were just as bigoted as anyone else toward Italians, Poles, Jews and so on.

I am reminded of my first years teaching up at Center, Colorado, which is spud country. Lots of the people there had Irish and German names. They were prejudiced towards Hispanics, which didn't sit well with me. I think also of a story from my early Santa Fe career. A girl told me her family members were *Spirish*. One-half of the Fort Union troops in 1870 were Irish or German-born. They worked on the railroads and in the mines. They often married local girls, who were also Catholic. There were old Irish immigrants, too, who came even in the 1700s. They tended to settle in the south, and because there were rarely a lot in one place, they became Presbyterians, which were dominant in that area. Consider Tara in *Gone with the Wind*. Only Maryland was Catholic, founded by John Carroll, an Irish Catholic. Over time, a few of those southerners came to the Sacramentos. One of them may have been one of the best agents the Mescaleros ever had, James A. Carroll, from 1902 to 1912. Remember that the big church at Mescalero is Catholic.

Let us consider a short list of Irish Americans, who have given much to the United States, and the side of life they affected: music— George M. Cohan, Bing Crosby, Tim McGraw and Gene Kelley; comedy—Jackie Gleason and Art Carney; literature—F. Scott Fitzgerald and Cormac McCarthy; architecture—Augustus St. Gaudens; Theater/ Acting—James Cagney, George Clooney, Ed Sullivan, Soirese Ronan and Grace Kelly; art—Georgia O'Keeffe; military service—George Gordon Meade, Audie Murphy, the Irish Brigade, and Stephen W. Kearney and Philip Sheridan, both of whom had much to do with bringing New Mexico into the Union and taming the west; and machinery—Henry Ford and Cyrus McCormick. I am also reminded that near Ruidoso is the village of San Patricio, made somewhat famous by Peter Hurd. It was named by an Irish Catholic priest.

So, as we celebrate the *Wearin' o' the Green*, let us think of the big picture and the philosophy underlying it. Life would be pretty boring without such people. Besides, I love the two pots of shamrocks I have in my house.

Spring is on the way, even if it is as tumultuous as the Irish ever were.

On an Economic Question

I took a trip to a different world in January. Up the Santa Fe Trail we went to Denver (not Kansas—sorry, Toto) to see friends. The greater Denver area seems to swim in money—not the case with the old coal fields and agricultural rural areas one traverses to get there. In fact, coal for power plants and minor steel production is now carried in very long trains from Wyoming. There were also a lot of homeless people camped in front of the state capitol. These discrepancies lead me to a question and an assignment. So, class, get out your notebooks and pens and prepare to write.

What would you do if you suddenly came into a large amount of money? Further, what would you buy? What would make you happy? What would you buy that I wouldn't? Who would you help? What fantasy would you try to fulfill? What would you need? Mull this over—even ruminate on it.

They say happiness is something money cannot buy. Who *they* are is unclear, but they are being irrational and simplistic. Money can't solve all the problems that we humans suffer, but it takes money to tackle most of them. Certain conditions humans suffer don't sound like fun to me, including both physical and mental illness. Not every person is equally fortunate in life nor does life fairly reward us all. I just finished an excellent book titled *The Feather Thief*. The greed evident in the story is disturbing. By the way, it begins in New Mexico. Your book club should read it.

Be prudent with your money—or, perhaps, Scottish. People who worry too much about it or try to make more often fall victim to scammers and lose it. Worrying about money you need and don't have isn't healthy either. Where is the happy medium? Anyway, you can only drive one vehicle at a time, be in one place at a time, eat one meal at a time and wear one outfit at a time.

In the movie *Mary Queen of Scots*, the royals exhibit their wealth through castles, food and clothing. What the film may be referring to is the fact that those with great wealth have no guarantee of happiness. They suffer like everyone else in a multitude of ways. They lose children, see their kids suffer, suffer diseases themselves, fail to create good in the world, suffer injustice and failure, and so on. Money cannot buy a lot of things.

So, I am glad to be home, safely ensconced in my warm nest with good, simple food and loved ones to share life with. We had an amazing experience in Sacramento in early March of rime frost coating the trees. All the oil money over in the Permian Basin couldn't buy that. Let the fantasies go. I guess my ego is sort of under control—as much as it can be for us peacocks and bucks.

On Contrails

In Santa Fe during the winter months, the colder air produces an amazing scene in the skies. There are a lot of clear, sunny days, and the blue yonder is etched with contrails, often up to a dozen at once. I like to guess where they are coming from and going. This requires a knowledge of geography and of maps and memory of my own travels. I didn't fly until I was almost 21. Last year, we flew four times, touching both coasts. I've been in about 40 airports, which is not much compared to some people I know. This must have some impact on our minds in terms of seeing the world around us.

Imagine a pre-Columbian Indian living anywhere inside New Mexico's mountain boundaries. He has not been outside his valley or basin and knows only that there may be other beings over the mountain, beings not to be trusted. One fine day he sees a white line coming over the mountain, moving toward him, and he hears a faint roar. What does he imagine? There is a true story comparable to this regarding Indians seeing sailing ships for the first time. He is probably shaking.

Travel educates. You know that yourselves. Air travel has vastly increased that education. However, some choose to be blind, as any teacher knows. We had a few hippie nutcases up here who called them *chem trails* and insisted it was a government plot to control us. (See my essay on motor vehicles.) They supposedly poison and otherwise kill us, but that didn't keep the hippies from driving beat-up, old, oil-burning vehicles.

Every so often a pair of contrails cross each other in an X or like a Christian cross. That gets our attention, and we wonder if we are being sent a message. Do any of you remember when we used to see V-2 rocket trails soaring up over White Sands Missile Range? They zigzagged because winds blow different directions at different altitudes. Mankind did not know much about all this until World War II bombing campaigns really opened up the sky. When bombers flying over Japan flew into the jet stream and started flying backwards, the crews may have felt like our hypothetical Indian for a moment.

Another memory I have is of the week after 9/11. There were no contrails in the sky, and I missed them. I saw two fighter jets overhead one time. Those sky-signs have become part of life, and they make me think about places I have been. They can deceive, especially in terms of where travelers are going. One time a flight from North Carolina home via Texas got cancelled due to mechanical issues, resulting in our being put on a plane for Las Vegas. We waved at the lights of Santa Fe as we flew by to the north, and we spent several wee morning hours playing the slots—the Scot in me kept us from investing too much. We arrived back in Albuquerque from the west about dawn.

Anyway, next time you see one, let your imagination take a trip. Bon Voyage.

On the American Revolution

A **PROGRAM IN** use to improve public school history curriculums is designed to get kids to think. It poses questions like, "Was the American Revolution really a revolution?" Most of us say, "Nonsense, of course it was!" It did create a new nation, although some thought it created 13 nations, and it took another war to resolve that issue. Some have called it a civil war. In that men from a given colony often fought on opposing sides, it was. Considering our love affair with the current Royal Family, I have to wonder if it was a family feud.

In this auspicious month of July, 243 years later, I would like to look at the problems the Americans faced in establishing their identity with flags and symbols. A serious revolution would call for radical changes, one would think. However, the human mind generally clings to the familiar, and there is such a thing as color psychology. That, in turn, has cultural components, some of which may be attached to geography. The most universal flag color is white, which seems to represent purity.

The English flag was white with a red St. George's cross. The Scots flew a blue field with a white St. Andrew's cross, which is called a saltire and looks like an X. The old Irish flag was white with a red St. Andrew's/Patrick's saltire. So, when the United Kingdom jelled in the early 1800s, all three were included on the Union Jack.

In 1775, the American colonists were all over the map. Some, called Tories, remained loyal to Britain. The others needed unity. Many of them still saw themselves as British and hoped for reconciliation; hence, they sewed a Union Jack over a corner of 13 red-and-white stripes: the first American flag. The King didn't cave, so Betsy did her job by replacing the crosses with 13 stars in a circle. *The Stars and Stripes* were born. But they did not have cell phones, TV or *People* magazine, and apparently the only word that went out was that the new flag was red, white, and blue and had stars and stripes. Try to imagine in your mind's eye one with stripes in the upper left corner, a blue body and 13 eight-pointed stars in a circle—or blue stars on a white field and red and blue stripes. How about a Union Jack in the upper right, red body and the words, *Liberty and Union,* across it? All of these existed.

As states were added over the years, stars were arranged in different patterns, and for a brief time, there were 15 stripes, but that obviously couldn't go on. In 1814, the term, *Star Spangled Banner,* was born. It seemed to solidify the design. The enemy were the Brits again, and some have argued that only at this point did the American Revolution end, although we would scuffle again in the 1860s. The states played with interesting images, too.

There were at least five variations of the snake flag. Thank God, we did not adopt that. New England liked green, so pine trees were on several flags. They also made one with a blue field, white stars and a green body. Rhode Island placed an anchor and the word, *hope,* on their blue-and-white banner, while South Carolina chose all blue with a crescent moon in the upper corner. Yet another echoed Patrick Henry with a minuteman and the phrase, *Liberty or Death.*

Considering cultural color psychology—and these are generalizations—northern Europe tends to red, white and blue. As one moves south, red, white and green are prominent. Africa likes green, yellow and red, while Asia leans toward red, white and yellow. Black, indicating passion, shows up on some Moslem flags, and, most notably, plays a role in the story of the German flag, a story unto itself.

In 1836, Texas created the lone star flag in red, white and blue. Well, duh! Several flags appeared when rebellion broke out in 1861. Virginia flew a blue one with a single white star. The initial banner was replaced with the *Stars and Bars*, which most people today don't know. The St. Andrew's saltire cross was only a battle flag. Remember that Lincoln refused to remove the Confederacy's stars from the old colors. Finally, I will tell you that the most iconic photograph in American history is the flag-raising on Iwo Jima in 1945. So, on the 4th, raise Old Glory, symbol of our indivisible republic with liberty and justice for all.

On Human Frailty
and the "Book of Job"

I HAD HIP replacement surgery in June, which made me very aware of the frailty of the human body and spirit. There is a mental pang when we cannot do our duties and others must carry us. We ask, "Why me? What did I do to deserve this?" Enter stage right my favorite book of the *Bible,* "Job," and following close behind, Satan, the Devil, Beelzebub, and Incarnate Evil. Things get complicated.

Life is tough, unpredictable and unfair. Most religions attribute suffering to our sins. Job seems to have committed no sins. It turns out that this event was a test dreamed up by Satan, and we are left wondering why an omniscient, omnipotent creator would allow such a thing. It is all a great mystery. Another thought creeps into play. Job is clearly a righteous dude, and the demon doesn't like him. Maybe it is that mean guys just like to see good people suffer. This, however, raises another question: does Satan control Jehovah?

Time to consider the definition of *allegory*: "Expression, by means of fictional figures and actions, truth or generalizations about human existence."

The body is fragile, imperfect and easily pained, so as we seek answers to our suffering, we forget that it is also an amazing entity. We want it to always be perfect, always at its best. Why can't we always win? Why must Charlie Brown's baseball team get pounded again? This once led to a Sunday comic strip which devolved into a theological dispute over the "Book of Job." When my junior year Alamogordo football team went 0-9-1, it didn't kill us.

I also know that the seeming promise of immortality touted by the medical/pharmaceutical alliance is a chimera, even if we have good insurance. I know, too, that my dream of staying 10 forever when my only responsibilities were going to school and cleaning the chicken coop—and I had no sense of girls—is a sweet dream.

A phrase comes to mind: "the patience of Job." It is wrong. He was rebellious and for good reason. He wanted simple answers, but in the end, he had to accept life, as we all do, even if we go down kicking and screaming. One blessing of this moment is my grandson, but even he must learn. He is teething.

Evil has always existed. Why? That is the way the world is and was for the ancient Hebrews. Surrounded by enemies and hostile nature, they needed answers and comfort. The *Bible* and its cousins try to provide this through proper behavior (at least toward one's own people) and through guardians like St. Michael and St. George with their swords fending off demons. Both, by the way, are patrons of military forces.

Because answers are not forthcoming, we must blame something or someone. What made me asymmetrical, which led to my current glitch in my getalong, i.e., hip? When in pain and anger, I can only assume it was the evil ones.

Part of our mystery is that in spite of evil and pain, life contains beauty, power, wonder, majesty, love and grace. Resignation and meek acceptance of and undeserved guilt about our pain serve no good purpose if they prevent us from questions and, thereby, inventing things like hip replacement surgery. Neither self-righteousness nor rebellion serves us if they leave us only with perpetual anger and insensitivity to the pain and needs of others. So, we are sort of caught on the Devil's horns, as it were. Job finally accepted his pain, passed the test and was rewarded.

A final thought: when we ask why evil exists, perhaps we need to see it as the definitive opposite of good—it is how we know what good is; otherwise, we would live sluggish, bland, blank, boring lives of blahness. We need the drama.

Postscript: Patience. It is hard to learn. About July 4th things got better, and by the 6th, I could drive. It was the patience that Job had to learn, which I did, too. One can't help but be thankful when things get better.

ON COLLEGE EDUCATION

IT IS TIME for the fall semester to start. This time of year, I think about personal history and that of family and friends. My parents' generation were the first in their families to go to college, and we were just expected to. In fact, in aggregate, we attended every old college in New Mexico except N.M. School of Mines (Tech), and my wife worked for the old St. Michael's College for 36 years.

What does a college education mean? This depends on the times. A Harvard graduate of 1870 would not match one from 1970. It also depends on the college. A degree from a technical school is not the same as one from a good liberal arts college. A structured curriculum is different from one which allows students to select all their courses. A fixed liberal curriculum is different from a fixed, narrow curriculum, which one might find at some religious schools.

Does an educated person mean being an expert in one field—or does it mean being broadly educated without expertise in any field? Does it mean having memorized a lot of facts—or having the ability to critically analyze facts well? Does it mean just having gone through a process? If the process is narrow in focus, rigid, and based on memorization, it is not the same as one which requires critical thinking, including creative, artistic processes.

Can college graduates communicate with each other uniformly on a higher level? Yes, and No. I always found communication difficult with my Uncle John, USMA class of '26, and I am sure my daughter, Franklin & Marshall class of '96, might say the same of me, University of New Mexico class of '64. The commonalities are somewhat small compared to the differences. Differences are reflected in biases and opinions. Clearly logical thinking would eliminate a lot of these differences. My conclusion is that either colleges don't produce many logical people, or human individual feelings and fears are too great for college to overcome them.

Abraham Lincoln and Harry Truman never went to college. They did OK, logically and philosophically speaking. People can educate themselves. Colleges are a business, a bureaucracy, a source of jobs and political institutions, whether they educate or not. They do educate, despite all these distractions, but let us not assume that a college education has any clearly definable meaning.

Regional differences have an effect, too. Early on, the North had three times as many schools as the South. Slavery stifled education; the slavocracy wanted ignorant whites beneath them. The early schools were religious most of the time, but the Protestants promoted education to teach their religious views, only to open the door to skeptical, liberal thinking. Urban life is educational, as is travel, both of which expose young people to other peoples and cultures. Rural life isolates, yet the rural person is learning things the urban soul loses. When rural kids go to A&M, they still should be expanding their horizons, however much it frightens the folks back home.

Should a school serve only one ethnic group, race or sex? Can education be provincial and still be good education? Debatable. Colleges which are narrow, which focus ethnically, religiously, racially or by gender, cannot produce the same education as diverse institutions. A portion of valuable learning at college has nothing to do with the classroom. In the humanities, especially, an imbalance will occur in all-female, all-Black, or all-Bohemian schools. I think the time is past when such schools are necessary.

People should get college credit for travel, reading, work experience, rehab, and military service. They should be able to get it with a minimum of bureaucratic hassle and nonsense. Neither should egotism on the part of college faculty get in the way. If we are going to give college credit for high school AP courses of questionable uniform value, then we should certainly give personal experience credit. A 30-year-old who has lived is more educated, if not as moldable, than any innocent 18-year-old.

Hail to the Alma Mater!

On the Winter Solstice

THAT TIME OF year is upon us—long nights, short days and cold weather! The world has changed and is about to again. That is what the cycle of seasons is about. Perpetual change and certain constants do battle in our minds. They befuddle, confuse, please and frighten us. Opposition implies conflict, yet we say opposites attract. Opposites can lead us to change our thinking, or they just harden our beliefs. Consider what never changing would mean. I can't say that swinging by vines from trees in a jungle, while in deadly fear of pythons on the ground, appeals to me.

At Christmastime, we tend to reflect on the year past and then welcome the New Year with faith that springtime will come, all symbolic of our hopes for a better future or fear of a worse one. Fate is in charge and will do with us as it pleases. It will not let us go backward, however. I think of several stories I have run across recently.

In preparing photos for the Tularosa Basin Historical Society, I noticed and pointed out to a young clerk helping me that the loggers in one had no chain saws, just 100 or so years ago. The photos are all black and white, taken with huge cameras and developed on glass plates like you have in your windows. I also realized that when I discovered these photos 38 years ago, I could not copy them on a copy machine. Now everyone and his dog has a cell phone camera, and we don't know where this is taking us.

In another case, I read a small, Buddhist-inspired piece of advice, purely by accident. The gist of it is that we should not dwell on our mistakes of the past. We should admit them and move on. I also heard an Irish song my wife was playing on a CD. It is titled "Isle of Hope, Isle of Love." Typical of Irish music, it has both sad and happy tones and lyrics. The basic theme is first about Ellis Island, where 17 million immigrants landed in America over a 51-year period and how they could never forget their homelands, despite dark events there. Then the song shifts to the very first to land, a 15-year-old girl named Annie Moore, for whom her new home is her future. The line, "'cause there's no future in the past when you're 15 years," is what caught my attention.

Later, I thought about why we study history and keep mementos of the past. While that line is true for almost any age, it is not for old folks who slip into dementia. Unfortunately, humans generally have trouble realizing the truth of it. This is the cause of much of our current angst and the negative culture of blame for our sorrows. The past is past. The only true way out is forward. I am reminded of the Marines trapped at Chosin Reservoir in Korea in the winter of 1950. They saw their retreat as a path to future victories and were not about to go to prison camps. They called it an advance in another direction.

I watch the progress of the sunsets through the year from my patio. It seems like the sun is zooming south now, so I do a little math. In early February, it will be back where it is now. There is hope.

So, I hope the Christmas season allows you to reflect on a good year past with memories you will long cherish. I must tell you, however, that the message of the season is that spring is coming, bringing another year full of memories, which only fate and time will reveal.

Merry Christmas and a Happy New Year.

ON A VIEW WITH HISTORY

OVER THE YEARS, I have driven south to Sacramento hundreds of times. Traveling south, when I am about 20 miles north of Carrizozo, I have a sense of a 200-degree arc view of a lot of history. The teacher in me demands that I tell my story, so, sit up class and pay attention.

The basic view is looking down the Tularosa Basin, and my first thought is that if I had been here early on the morning of July 16, 1945, I would have seen a huge flash just over Oscura Mountain. The government would have told me later that it was just a bomb dump exploding accidentally, like the munitions train up at Taiban the previous November. A month later, I would have learned about Trinity (not Alamogordo, as too many historians say).

A ways beyond that is Victorio Peak, named for an Apache leader who raided through the area in 1878-81. Pursued by the cavalry, he moved on into Mexico where the Mexican army got him. Of course, the magnificent view of Sierra Blanca on the Mescalero Reservation reminds me of the long wars between Spain and Mexico—the U.S. Buffalo Soldiers included—against the various Apache peoples. A slight swing to the east calls up Fort Stanton, a major post in those wars.

In 1862, the Fort was captured by the Confederate Texas army, which crossed the Basin from Mesilla and then became part of Kit Carson's campaign in 1864-66. It later housed tuberculosis victims and, briefly, German and Japanese American prisoners in World War II. It also served for a time as a correctional facility. Today, it is a museum. The view across that gap north of Sierrra Blanca means we must consider the biggest story of all, the one many serious historians have grown weary of: Billy the Bad Boy!! I won't go into that with you.

Instead, we should consider how Lincoln got its name. It was made official in 1873, in honor of Abraham Lincoln. Before that, Spanish-American settlers had briefly established a settlement there, as they had at Tularosa and La Luz. Earlier, Spaniards explored the area in order to settle the mountain streams, but they could not control the Apaches. If we swivel our heads a little more to the east, we are looking toward White Oaks, where W.H. Weed set up shop and sent his name south into the Sacramentos. Miners were all over the basin, but only a few small lodes of gold were found.

The lust for gold and other natural resources propelled events. Weed was then in Lincoln County, and raising livestock was the one enterprise which could be pursued over the whole region. Enter the two Alberts and Oliver. Albert Fountain and Albert Fall were political rivals in southern New Mexico. Both were Union veterans and lawyers. Oliver Lee was a Texas cattleman. In 1892, Fountain went with his son to Lincoln to take testimony from several Weed men regarding brand-changing, supposedly by Lee. Fountain and son disappeared near the White Sands. Lee was accused and acquitted, defended by Fall. Fall did well: he bought the Three Rivers Ranch beneath Sierra Blanca, tried to exploit the Mescalero Reservation, became state Senator and Secretary of the Interior and went to prison over oil.

In the late 1890s, railroads began to enter the Basin. They needed water, coal and ties, which could be found in the mountains. Now, when I make the trip down, I see very long trains of vegetable oil, coal containers and auto-carrying cars. They don't run on steam anymore, so the water can help grow nuts. Another glance to the east, where a rail line once ran, reminds me that Smokey the Bear was born in the Capitans, where in 1950 he got singed in a forest fire, healed, and was taken to the national zoo as a symbol of fire prevention. The Basin is the only place I have ever seen dust devils, and the winds of spring and fire do not go well together.

Far to the south, on a clear day, I will see the Franklin Mountains. They will bring to mind Pancho Villa, who kept Fort Bliss busy and supposedly stayed at Cloudcroft once. I will remember Pete Hansen, too. He came from Denmark, was a cowboy in the San Andres, served with the cavalry at Fort Bliss and married Nellie Shields at Sacramento. He was sort of a Eugene Manlove Rhodes character. My memory sees rocket trails, too, soaring up from the White Sands Missile Range, where the American space program began with all those German scientists, whose kids were my classmates at Alamogordo High School. Sometimes the rockets went astray. Jim Godley showed us the wreckage of one above the tunnel. That brings me to looking over my shoulder as I approach Carrizozo, just in case any UFOs are following me.

I am sure there are more stories and characters to mention, but this will do for one trip. The test is on September 16, the real Mexican Independence Day. Adios.

On Philosophy

THIS WHOLE EXERCISE is about philosophy, the search for truth. I didn't do well in college philosophy courses. The subject involved too many names and new words for my feeble mind. I kept trying to reduce it all to plain, common-sense English, while trying to keep St. Augustine, Hegel, Descartes, Marx and so on all straight. I'm still trying.

In reading some Eastern philosophy recently, I noticed that it really isn't that different from Western ideas. Humans all raise the same questions and think the same thoughts about them. They just come up with different, sometimes contrasting answers. It takes all kinds to make a world.

Perhaps we do not know enough about the brain yet to understand why there can be so many conflicting explanations for the puzzles of life. Anything from color blindness to a head injury to pre-natal care to childhood experience to ignorance could explain the views of an individual. Mass blindness, mass hysteria and mass denial are a bit more difficult to understand.

I do think philosophers have a duty to make their ideas clear, concise and simple. Most of them do not do their duty. There is an element of intellectual snobbery at work among them, along with a desire for power, the power of the priesthood.

The snobbery comes out in the form of putting down clichés or aphorisms. These are too simple in the eyes of the intellectually arrogant, who fear a loss of personal status as well as a loss of power. Philosophy must be kept arcane. The movie critic is an example of this behavior. In the end, only you can decide what appeals to you. I am defining philosophy as a matter of opinion, not as gospel truth.

Even truths held by majorities have often proven to be wrong. The old "everybody knows" syndrome doesn't cut it. Simple does. This requires close attention to use and meaning of language, by the way.

If you cannot get the idea across to an average, healthy six-year -old, something is wrong with your approach. Is it any wonder that those in power across the ages have sought to keep the masses in a state of childish ignorance? More bothersome is the scenario in which the masses choose to accept this status. I can understand the desire to remain a child to a point, but the behavior ain't normal beyond that point.

Could it be that having to really think gives the masses a headache? The headache stems in part from the fact that there is often no clear answer to the *whys* of our existence. As a result, there are many different philosophies. The paths to the truth are many, and humans in general do not deal well with ambiguity. Still, we must teach that there is more than one way to skin a cat.

ON MIGRATION AND MUTATION

SOME YEARS AGO, I designed a potential course for high school or college titled "Migrations and Mutations." It was intended to explain how the U.S. developed across time. It was based on my experience as a history teacher across four decades.

Students sometimes asked why people behaved so badly in the past, and there was often a tone of either victimization or of shared blame in their voices, which I did not like. I created a set of three propositions and a question. To wit:

1. The world would be better off if humans never left their place of origin.
2. The world would be better off if humans never invented or created anything new.
3. The world would be better off if humans never had to change.
4. What does it mean to be human?

Often the students would look at me like I was crazy. One very bright young lady nailed it, however. She said, in relation to proposition 1, "You mean the primordial ooze?" It is about our problem with change. Change is often traumatic, and not every change is good. Why this is so is a great mystery. It should be a role of modern education to help us find our way.

For that to happen, we have to ask, "Why?" We need to be grounded in geography, sociology, psychology and anthropology. We need a sense of time and proportion. We desperately need a larger vocabulary. We need to know where we came from, while understanding that the past is past. We need to think deeply about morality, war, epidemics, natural disasters, economic stresses, scientific change and revolution. We need to think about why these things happen.

Humans suffer fear, paranoia and tribalism. They need food, shelter and to be able to procreate. They have also evolved to need answers. They have brains. Another mystery is why change can happen so suddenly and in certain places. Why did the Industrial Revolution begin in England? Geography is part of the answer. Climate, food, loss of resources or having resources can be part of the answer. Revolutions are not just political.

Immigrants are a big part of this story. I often write about them. Their role was one of the early lessons I created for my students, even before *Roots* happened. I also tied this to the Pledge of Allegiance and the matter of patriotism. Politics and governance change. I have no desire to be ruled by a king, thank you, and neither do a lot of other people. This is a big part of what made American culture unique. It also led to conflicts of other sorts.

Had there never been conflict there would be no heroes. How boring that would be! Perhaps one of our human needs is for drama and humor. Life might not be worth living otherwise. So, people move about the earth creating vibrant new societies out of various conflicts.

The lesson plan I created is much longer than this rumination. You will find references to many of these topics in my other essays. The world keeps spinning and changing.

About Books

By the book. The gospel truth. People of the Book. Bookish. Bookworm. Humans have a thing or two about books. They both fear and respect them. You can make book on it.

Books contain secrets, formulae, magic spells and other esoteric knowledge. They contain facts, truth, right and wrong. They can be dangerous or nonsensical. Bookish people have power and are not to be fully trusted by the masses. Our long relationship with the book has conditioned us in ways which are not always healthy. We often put too much faith in the book. I have observed, over the years, behaviors most bothersome about books. Students may function well if given a textbook, which they have only to read and memorize non-analytically. Given any other material, these students may freak out, puzzled by the form of the material without regard to its content. Having to analyze it destroys their equilibrium. Out of this, we get the rote memorization of essentially useless information, which society sets much store by.

Principals and parents like textbooks, too, for somewhat similar reasons. If it is in the book, it is real, safe, repeatable and not challenging to them, either. God forbid that kids should know more than their elders.

Today, we presume the problem to be that kids don't read enough—they would rather play with computers or watch MTV. I believe as many kids read as ever did because there were always many who did not read despite broad literacy. Some cannot read easily, others not at all. For many, reading is tedious, boring. In an 1891 Kipling poem entitled "Tomlinson," the main character says, "O this I have read in a book," as he pleads his case to St. Peter for admission to heaven. Peter replies, "Ye have read? What have ye done?" Now, I plead guilty on that count: I have read a thousand plus books, but I worry that I have not lived sufficiently. We cannot all be like Theodore Roosevelt, who read, acted constantly and wrote 20 books—my point being that some people can draw life out of good books (the name of a wonderful bookstore in Santa Fe at one time), and others must experience life. Blesséd are those who can do both.

Books are tools. Tools define mankind. We love our tools, love the very feel of them. Some love books, others do not. Perhaps the issue is most serious for those who do not consider books as their tools. We all tend to be in awe of those who use any tool well when we cannot. They have power over us. We must depend on them for satisfaction of various needs, knowing we are helpless on our own.

I think I am on the verge of contradicting myself. I argue too well that some can interpret books beyond an elementary level. If this is true, those who deal in books have a moral obligation to be honest and compassionate with those who do not, the same ethos we expect of all tradesmen, and we are all tradesmen.

My challenge to educators is to not depend on textbooks. Do not surrender to the easy out. Read! Read all the time. Read eclectically—broaden yourself and broaden your students. Make them read above their level. Increase their vocabulary, at least, thereby increasing their knowledge of the world. Words embody ideas. But never teach that the truth lies in a book. Mankind has suffered enough from that lie.

On Tilting at Windmills

I DROVE ACROSS the Jornada del Muerte today and started noticing windmills, lots of them in that vast, desolate plain surrounded by mountains. Don Quixote de La Mancha came to mind. Why are we humans so willing to do battle with fears which are unreasonable, to make giants and monsters out of small, insignificant things? The Bomb was first tested on that Plain. In the long run, a host of lesser unpleasant things could overwhelm one: Apaches, thirst, the sun, starvation, dust, rattlesnakes. Why worry about a piddly nuclear weapon?

I wondered if being a child of this region causes me to see the world in a different perspective—the sky is so large, the distances so great, one's view unhindered. Could it be that a windmill is just a windmill, a bomb just a bomb, our fears far less than we make them? But there is another side to being Quixotic. It is the desire to have purpose and meaning, attained only by dint of service in the name of Good against Evil. The fear of nihilism may drive us to crazy behavior. It has also been said that the vastness of La Mancha drives men crazy. How appropriate that this plain is named "The Journey of Death," for is not the journey of life a journey towards death?

In a world devoid of man-made things, windmills could take on extra importance. Man can cope with his own creations for he thinks he can control them. The Creator's creation is another matter. Windmills are benign aids to man in his fight against the cruel vagaries of nature. Why joust with them, then? This must be a major literary statement made long before Freud. Cervantes and Shakespeare were contemporaries and were proto-psychologists, well aware of the human proclivity for being blind to reality. They knew that humans tend to see what they want to see—or to see what is happening inside their heads, rather than in front of their eyes.

I have felt no desire to go galloping after each windmill I saw and have been quite content to sail by and away from them, on to more pleasant places. No Knight Errant I!

On "Chong Wang, a Terrible Name for a Cowboy"

I just saw an ad for a John Wayne DVD collection of western movies, which reminded me of this great line from *Shanghai Noon*. It also reminded me of how sick some elements of society can be. There is a lot of delusional denial going on when people put up a statue of a movie star dressed as a cowboy, then worship it as though he were a hero.

Long ago, I used to have 8th graders list their heroes. Every year John Wayne made the list a few times. I finally realized that I needed to preface the assignment with a discussion of what *hero* means as opposed to *idol* or *star*. Once I cleared that up, movie stars, rockers, and Nixon disappeared, replaced wonderfully by parents and other family members.

Simple facts: John Wayne was never a soldier. He avoided service in World War II when he could have gone. He was not a cowboy, either; he was an actor. How sick is it that a body of people choose to believe a fiction, an act? We can't even call it myth because there is no kernel of truth to it.

The statue was created by his worshipers in Orange County, California. Maybe that says enough. Denial isn't in Egypt—it's in la-la land. Possibly Wayne's best piece of work was *The Quiet Man*. I wonder if his idolaters even know it. Since he played neither soldier nor cowboy in it, they would be likely to block it out of their consciousnesses.

Chong Wang, indeed, Pilgrim!

On the Greatest Human Illness

A POLL WOULD undoubtedly place AIDS, cancer, bird flu, heart disease, drug abuse and violence at the top of the list. The greatest illness would not make the list. This would happen because the illness blinds us to its existence and its nature.

This illness has names: hypocrisy, inconsistency, denial, enabling, dogmatic stubbornness, irrationality, and excessive emotionalism are among them. The disease is our refusal to see what we do not want to see.

I am reminded of a historic example. Southern slave owners and northern racists screamed loudly and fought viciously over the attack on their rights, while conveniently ignoring the fact that they were denying these same precious, sacred rights to millions of slaves. The hypocrisy of the claim to be defending states' rights, while ignoring the existence of slavery as an issue, was—and is—a monstrous sickness.

This behavior is repeated throughout history. Why? I have no doubt that our fears related to survival are a major piece of the puzzle. We are always whistling in the dark, pretending all is well, posing bravely, our manhood intact. Can we not survive without this behavior? Perhaps we need the challenge the fear creates in order to address the problem.

Eventually, we get it right—at great cost.

There is that mystery of people succeeding because they refuse to admit defeat or failure. I don't know how to assess the legitimate balance of this equation. When should we know that it is time to quit or change? There seems to be some logic involved in our illness, just as there is in a small level of paranoia or neurosis. These are survival mechanisms.

There is that human tendency to think that if we think or speak evil, we will jinx ourselves; ergo, not speaking of evil protects us from it. Could it be that our denial behavior is rooted in ancient fears based on lack of understanding of the natural world? If so, that world still contains enough unanswered mysteries to keep us in fear.

Consider how we scapegoat when things go wrong. Fear breeds prejudice, prejudice breeds scapegoating, and scapegoating breeds hatred and violence. FDR was right about fear. How, then, do we overcome it? This is preeminently the time to speak the truth, the whole truth, frankly and boldly. Sadly, I've noticed that even well-educated, supposedly confident people too often cannot do this. Our background, education and lenses are too firmly in place. Short of a wet mop, a 2x4, or a Great Depression, this background and these lenses will not get out of the way of our commonsense logic. I think this is why it is easier to presume God loves us and will take care of us if we just believe—and perhaps God will. God's will be done.

On the Witches'
Brew of Personality

It comes to me today that personality is a mixture of heredity, over which we have no control, and upbringing, over which we have no control, and what we attempt to make of the first two components through our supposed will power. I say *supposed* because I have serious doubts that we have free will. I don't question that we make decisions to change our lives—that we may, in fact, do so in limited ways—but I seriously doubt that we can really re-create ourselves from what we are to begin with.

In the case of heredity, we are doomed by whatever set of genes came down to us. If we are outgoing, charming, intelligent and charismatic—great! If we are shy, middling and unattractive—tough! If the latter tries to be the former person, it will be apparent that he is a fake. Literature is replete with stories to the contrary: *Cinderella, My Fair Lady, The Prince and the Pauper* and so on. They all fail, however, if put to the scientific tests of genetics and childhood training. Eliza Doolittle was too far along to be remodeled that much by the veneer of language.

Personality is very much about how we are molded as children, but it is also about the clay itself. You cannot make a silk purse out of a sow's ear, nor a racehorse out of a mule. Heredity aside, most people can be taught a modicum of manners, poise, proper behavior and cour-age, much of it by drill and threat of punishment or embarrassment. That rote learning will never match the natural poise some people are born with.

Personality trips up highly intelligent people and allows modest souls to slide through life. In fact, personality is the heart of Greek tragedy—the flawed man, who, for all of his talent, creativity or cour-age, ultimately shoots himself in the foot. We do judge others on the basis of how smooth they are—no wonder we are so easily scammed.

I guess what I am suggesting is that we should ease up on the idea that we can form personality and accept things as they are. This means becoming more tolerant of the rotten personalities, too, for they are a necessary part of the brew.

On Events Not of Our Choosing

I HAD AN interesting conversation today with a Nambe Pueblo girl about to enter her senior year at Yale. She commented that the Indians were not immigrants and, therefore, did not choose to be part of the great American experiment. The honor was forced upon them.

Well, that naturally set off my philosophy and history alarms. All human beings are forced by circumstances they didn't choose into places they didn't choose. Fate and circumstance chose for them. No one is immune. So, sorry, but I must once again insist that Indians are human.

The vast majority of immigrants were forced to come here by circumstances they did not choose—ask the Irish, the East European Jews, the Pilgrims and Amish, the Vietnamese, the Italians and Poles. It was not a pleasure cruise. (See my *Migrations and Mutations* essay for a more complete look at this fact of history.)

We didn't choose to be born in the first place, let alone choose the set of genes and the body of culture forced upon us by random nature. We must stumble through life dealing with the cards we were dealt. Of course, I, too, am guilty of looking heavenward and wailing, "Why me, God? What did I do to deserve this?" I'm afraid I am human.

Isn't it funny that this young woman, Yale-educated (which I am not), totally computer literate (which I am not), faced with a life of great possibilities is still mired in the goo of discontent, victimization and blame. I hope I planted a few seeds in her very capable mind.

A Jeremiad on the Notion of Reconciliation

Reconciliation: 1. "to restore friendship and harmony."

                                    2. "in the Catholic Church, the sacrament of penance."

Penance: "an act to show sorrow or repentance for sin."

JEREMIAH 32 IN the *Bible* refers to "the sins of the father." This quote is a primitive explanation of why the Hebrews were punished by war and exile. It could as easily apply to the Navajo as to Europeans. It is a total violation of the United States Constitution and judicial system—and of common sense, for that matter. It smacks of blood feuds and blood guilt.

No man or woman can guilt me for transgressions committed by our predecessors, and no people on this earth are guiltless of transgressions, so grow up people and get on with life, preferably in the sense of definition 1 of *reconciliation*.

Everyone and every group suffer. It is part of the human condition. Unfortunately, we have developed cultures to make us feel better, and far too many of us have bought into them, either as victims or victimizers. It is a rotten idea, it damages our society, and it does not in the end heal our wounds. We have to heal ourselves. The prayer says, "Forgive us our trespasses as we forgive those who trespass against us."

If we are to reconcile with each other in the truest and best sense of the Webster definition stated above, then let us bring to a screeching halt the accusatory whining, blaming, scapegoating, and guilting that too many of us are too good at.

I have spoken!

On Sports

It is a perfect fall Saturday—sun and blue sky, cool air—football weather. Across the land, college teams are going at each other. The World Series is upon us, too, although it should already be finished. To make matters worse, basketball and hockey are already happening, and it isn't their season yet.

I find it difficult to watch games anymore on TV or live. The Series is of some interest—competing are two teams which have never played against each other before— one is in its first-ever Series competition. An old fellow, Clemens, is pitching for Houston, and the White Sox go way back in time. A little tug at the heart is there, but much worn out. . .sad.

I'm a dinosaur. That is all there is to it. I want the good old days, even if they never were. There was something of purity in them that has been besmirched by commercialism. The game cannot be played truly well because the product might not sell. The fans are to blame in large part. They don't know the game and don't want it played at its best. They only want "bread and circuses." My God! The shadow of Rome hangs over us.

I coached once upon a time over a period of 17 years in four different sports. I don't think anyone thought I was particularly good. I doubt that I was much of a salesman. My favorite sport to coach was track and field, even if my heart was in football. At least I've been in the fray, so I can criticize with some degree of validity.

Sports are institutionalized war—tribal war, mostly—so I reckon the explosive growth of sports over the last half century is a good thing if it reduces real conflict. There are too many cheerleaders and armchair generals for my taste, though. Could it be just age, less testosterone that makes me content here on the porch writing instead of being in the stands or before the altar of television? Is it perhaps not a good thing to know too much, to be too discerning, too discriminating? Have I become a tad too cosmopolitan to engage in tribal hysteria? Could it be that I always, from childhood, knew that they really were just games, and silly ones at that, not worth the emotional investment so many put into them?

Yet on crossword puzzles I can call up out of the mists of time the names of baseball players, a game I neither played nor followed as a child. I still love the old accounts of Damon Runyon, Grantland Rice and Bill Stearn. I love *Field of Dreams* and *Chariots of Fire*. They each have an element of something I would wish for on Aladdin's Lamp—to see my father at age 18 set the high school 100-yard dash record, to see him run for a touchdown, to hear him sing the lead in HMS Pinafore at Santa Fe High. How thrilled I was a year after I wrote this essay to discover that he traveled all the way to Philadelphia by train, in 1941, to see his brother, RJ, play in the Army-Navy game nine months before I was born.

I believe that cultural literacy requires some knowledge of sports and that in one's youth, participation is a good thing. I was nothing special in school sports, but I had some fun. I thought that was the point of games. What got lost? The sports page in *The New Mexican* in the 1920s was only part of one page. Today, it is a whole multi-paged section. In the Sunday *Denver Post*, it is of frightening magnitude. Sports has grown. Television is partly responsible for the woes I feel about games. Radio and newsreels of yore did not come close to the impact of television. The country has grown, too. Whereas all the pro teams were once in the northeast quadrant of the country, today they are in all corners. Florida colleges were nobodies then. Today they are dominant. When Moriarty High School beats several Albuquerque public schools, you know something has happened.

In 1906, Michigan played nine games. Three were against their own reserves, one against their alumni, three home games, including Case, and two road trips by train. The team consisted of 14 men. The reserves numbered 30, who did not travel nor did they necessarily suit up for games. None were Black. When my own University of New Mexico flew to play Montana in 1935 or so, the first team to do so, the world changed.

A child-centered culture changed things, too, beginning in the 1950s. More kids—girls included—entered sports. Unfortunately, part of the impetus for this was adults' needs for vicarious success and excitement. This culminated in the rash of shootings of Texas coaches and cheerleader moms and so on. Down there, sports take on religious dimensions; this is how we know Jesus really had short hair—a high school football coach proclaimed it! Old tribal rivalries began to be played off the field, and the rivalries had to be cancelled. The Santa Fe High School-St. Michael's competition had to be put on hold for several years.

Even mascots became an issue. Most people today have no idea that the reason Santa Fe High students call themselves the Demons is because it reflects the totally natural and historically correct relationship between the Devil and St. Michael. At one time, St Mike's students were called the Saints. Check out your basic iconography, dudes. It all goes back to the original games. At least Santa Fe Indian School still has the good sense and the guts to call themselves the Braves! Lady Braves is a little dubious, but the alternative just won't do. Pojoaque, the Elks, has the same problem. I digress.

Money! It would be easy to blame corporate America and its TV minions for all the ills attendant to sports, but they are only obeying the law of supply and demand. The fans are going to have to take some of the heat. The fans range from small, poor children to very rich, old alums. They are willing to pay for—or steal—sports gear, logos, players and prestige. The egos of sports team owners are legendary. A lot of this is economics. In *Brave New World*, Huxley noted the tendency to push games/sports because they require apparatus. It was the Great Depression, and the economy needed stimulation.

Schools regularly get put on probation because of the stupid behavior of alumni. Athletes get out of control vis a vis their egos, whether in regard to how much money they make, how much playing time they get, or what they think they can get away with in general. Eight-year-olds already specializing as wide receivers and 10-year-old girls emulating Oakland cheerleaders make me ill.

Pro salaries paid to grown men to play with various funny-shaped balls and sticks are sick. There is no kinder word for it. The behaviors of high school and college stars are sick when they step outside the bounds of propriety because they think their stardom makes them special. The bad behavior of fans is sick. A society that places more value on the slim possibility of being an NBA star than on becoming an educated citizen is unhealthy. It is a terrible thing to waste a child's mind in such ways.

Now that I have worked up a good rant, let me provide examples of how sick society has become in terms of ignorance and denial. Good football and good basketball demand good defense. Scores of 42 to 28 do not indicate much defense at all. The best defense is a good defense which does not allow the opponent to score at all. A good offense, which lends to good defense, is one which is controlled, eats up the clock and scores. Fifty passes a game does not qualify. A team which loses by scores like 35 to 32 is not playing defense and it loses. A team with a 6-6 win-loss record should not be going to bowl games.

The fans want a winner, but even more, they want to be thrilled by high scores. I would love to see my Alma Mater have an 11-0 season, scoring 77 points to its opponents zero. I am, of course, the only one in town to understand the obvious logic of this idea. Bah! "Bread and circuses!" Schools and pros alike pander to this fan demand to the ultimate detriment of sport. The pros are a bunch of mercenaries and can do what they want, but schools ought to do better.

While I am at it, society is obsessed with the concept of being number one. This has become the essence of the sickness. Now it shows up in a host of asinine, so-called reality shows on TV. Crowning champions is something of a joke when the numbers do not support the crown. The BCS college rating system for football indicates just how warped we've gotten. We don't need college football national champions. There are only about 30 teams likely to be able to compete, anyway. If the rest of the colleges had any collective guts, they would can the whole system and alienate those 30 teams—let them play each other and call it the minor leagues. Money raises its head again.

Bless Division III for maintaining some semblance of real sports. I still check the scores each Sunday morning in fall—old loves die hard, an obvious psychological truth this essay proves by its length. Knox, Franklin & Marshall and Rice aren't big winners, but they play the game. I know the Lobos will perennially break my heart.

I bought a football in Sam's Club the other day. It felt right. Life goes on.

ON NATURE

NATURE IS RED of tooth and claw. Nature is our only proof of a deity. Nature is beautiful from sea to shining sea. Mother Nature is a mean goddess. Will the real Nature stand up and be recognized? Nature includes all of life on this planet—the environment and the behavior of all things in it. We must be in awe of it and respect its power. We should be able to draw sustenance from it, spiritual as well as physical. We ought not romanticize it too much, and we ought to recognize the fact that man has always been at war with it.

I like to rhapsodize about nature as much as the next guy, but I am more honest about the relationship I have with nature than are many people. She is fun to look at—not so fun to be assaulted by. She is fun to view from a cozy shelter or during good weather while well-fed and healthy—not so fun when being frozen, baked, sickened or starved by her.

There is a lot of irrational emotion out there about nature, harmony with her and all that nonsense involving how certain people have a better relationship with her than others do. In fact, religion—old and new—has arisen largely out of mankind's effort to propitiate nature, which is always trying to kill him. Read "Job"; it is all about the power of nature.

I think the best we can do is to enjoy the view, be as careful as we can be, and realize that man and nature will never be fully compatible—pretty much like most marriages. Consider, too, that nature has the edge. Nothing more to say.

ON BEAUTY

A. Beauty is in the eye of the beholder
B. Beauty is as Beauty does
C. Beauty is only skin deep
D. All of the above

IT WOULD SEEM that certain magazines can tell us who the 50 or 100 most beautiful people in the world are. Even better, a panel of judges can pick Miss America, not that we always agree with them. Are we shallow, confused, or both? How can we buy into such nonsense?

There are cultural standards for aesthetics. Each culture has its own set. That old Greek, Plato, spent a lot of time arguing that there was a perfect, ideal form of everything. This evidently shows up in Greek sculptures of nude males and females. I remember a museum in Copenhagen filled with such pieces done in the neo-Greek period circa 1810. They got boring fast, much the way *Playboy* centerfolds do. The statuary in Frogner Park in Oslo was much more interesting. It was based on real people—old, young, sagging, taut—the works. I have always found the Platonic argument hard to buy, though I accept the idea of classic, timeless forms of beauty. Even those are dependent on a sort of democratic process—majority rules but cannot tyrannize the minority.

The gods like to play with us, and we confuse the feelings their little games arouse with beauty. The gods gave us sex. Thank God for Miss Congeniality, a small concession to something other than raw sexuality. Females are obvious victims of this confusion. From little girls to mature women, too many tears, too much energy and money are spent on insecurities about beauty. Too many of them give up too easily. And the gods are sitting there on the mountain above the aspens, enjoying the view and chuckling over that fool, Hill, thinking he's one of those dudes like Plato or Confucius.

Men worry about looks, but more of them suffer silently. The narcissists may look good, but they can be a pain in other ways. All this might not be such a problem if we were more honest with our language and called things what they really are. I should like to see magazines feature not the 50 most beautiful, but just 50 beautiful people, and then perhaps feature 50 beautiful dogs, 50 beautiful mountains, 50 trees, and so on. Don't pretend to be democratic about it either; you cannot let people vote and expect to find the truth. Stop the silliness.

It would be a fun, science fair project if a magazine published 50 beautiful personalities chosen by a panel, then let the readers vote to see what level of agreement occurs between panel and readers. Some hurt feelings might result among the panel and nominees, except for Miss Congeniality. She isn't allowed to exhibit any jealousy or other real emotions.

Now I am reminded why beauty is only skin deep. In most cases, that is all we see. Our first impressions are what we have to deal with. So, I say, "What a beautiful woman," not knowing that she is the evil bitch of the Western world. I say, "What a beautiful dog." Same problem. I say, "What a beautiful house," never knowing what horrors occur inside. I say, "What a beautiful landscape." We do this a lot in New Mexico, forgetting how harsh and unforgiving it usually is.

Beauty is in the eye of the beholder. We each are a mass of nerve ganglions served by biochemical formulas, which are conditioned by environment, and each of us is unique. Hence, our notions of beauty will inevitably lead to debate, forums and barroom brawls. I had an Aunt named Dollie. She would say, "She's so ugly, she's cute." Right on, Aunt Dollie, rest your beautiful soul.

On Overpopulation and the Myth of Sustainability

TIME **MAGAZINE DOES** it regularly—assaults us with the faces of starving Africans, with a planet suffering the throes of global warming and with the wonders of Chinese capitalism. It expends many pages telling how to save lives from diseases and how to save the planet from greenhouse emissions, but not one drop of ink is spent addressing the most serious issue of all: overpopulation. While this may just reveal another serious disease loose in the world—denial and delusion—I am also herewith accusing *Time* and others of sheer gutlessness. Maybe they are afraid of a decline in their subscription and advertiser lists. We shall kill even more of these too many people with loving kindness.

Hill's Overpopulation Formula is simple: divide population into resources and you get a number.

$$\text{Standard of Living} = \text{Resources} \div \text{Population}$$

Since resources are finite, the number can only get smaller as population grows. There are little factors which make this calculus more complex, but for the sake of our exposition, let us keep it simple. Now, if we divide up the wealth that the U.S., Western Europe and Japan have created among all God's children, what would we have? Six billion plus poor people!

It isn't human nature to accept abject poverty if an alternative is possible. Monks don't count—they are not normal humans. The rest of the world wants to be like us, not the other way around. I first became aware of this issue 40 years ago as a college student. The world then had half the number of people it has now. Too many people aren't listening. In our society, it is the religious literalists who obstruct a solution, all in God's name, of course. I rail at the arrogance of their presuming that they speak for God.

In other parts of the world where the problem is more serious, Kipling was right: "How dare we bring them from their loved Egyptian night?" If they will not learn and curse us at every turn for asking them to, at what point does our obligation to do anything for them end?

I saw a cheesy film titled *Blood Suckers* last summer. The plot? Intergalactic vampires threaten civilization and must be stopped by a team of vampire hunters. A bleeding-heart earth woman defends the vampires because they cannot help being products of their culture and heredity. The evil vampire leader finally kills her because she cannot deliver the goods—the weapons technology which civilization has created, a technology his backward culture cannot begin to build. He wants it to conquer and ravage others. Ironically, he isn't willing to learn any more than he already knows. Sound familiar? Fortunately for the viewer, the hunters kill him.

I think this is a highly underrated movie in terms of its message. If the world wants what we have, then the world is by golly going to have to change. Otherwise, quit whining, back off, go live your miserable lives and don't bother us. Harsh? Call it tough love.

If the underdeveloped world starts working on its population growth now, it might have some chance. If not, nature will very likely take care of the problem, and it won't be pretty. No medical aid should be dispensed hereafter without birth control included, and the complainers be damned because they are damning us all. I notice Al Gore wimped out on the issue, too, in his movie because he did not emphasize the overpopulation issue.

We could live more simply, I suppose, but human nature does not take easily to starving, freezing, baking and general suffering. Our dilemma is that all members of a growing population cannot have a high standard of living.

A related notion the press pushes is sustainability. I do not think sustainability is possible in the face of the issues above. There are limits, and too many people don't want to face them. It's sort of like speed limits and the guys driving down the interstate at 110 mph. There are no limits.

On Indiana Jones and his Problem with Snakes

Last night, we saw the latest Indiana Jones flick, which has the obligatory snake scene. Snakes seem to be the only thing he fears. Well, I opened the front door this morning, and there lay a 20-inch or so gopher or bull snake just waiting to enter. I told the little devil to be off—he curled up and hissed at me. I left it in its hiding place under a pot. This is Spanish Market weekend, and among the most creative works to appear there year after year are carvings of Michael the Archangel doing battle with the Devil in serpentine forms. They are among my favorite works.

In the *Dragons of Eden*, Sagan contends that the very center of our brain—the first, most primitive part of it—is the serpent brain. It is tiny and only capable of reacting to the most fundamental needs. It is where the seat of our paranoia lies, the reaction to perceived danger. Snakes strike because they are hungry or afraid. How very human! He also says dreams of snakes are one of the most common to the human species.

I used to kill snakes as a young boy until someone told me I shouldn't. I still don't like them but have begun to tolerate them. I even found myself eventually studying non-poisonous types. I realized that they are very afraid of me and other large animals—afraid to the point of being pitiable. Some Spanish carvers capture this pitiful quality well in the serpent St. Michael is poised to destroy.

The non-thinking, always paranoid snake brain offends us because it is the source of most of our bad and stupid behavior. We don't like to be reminded that we all too often behave like dangerous snakes. Our fears make us strike out, make us hide, make us sneaky, make us threatening and make us pitiful, cringing creatures.

In the ongoing battle between good and evil, is not the battle often between our own worse and better natures, individually and collectively? We have a much larger brain than a snake. We can think; we think. The trouble is we so often don't think. We act and react. However, we, unlike the snake as far as we know, can feel shame. After we act too precipitously and are wrong, we suffer great feelings of shame. Our esteem is at stake. So, we have the essence of conscience, the ability to be contrite, to seek atonement. Is it not interesting that we view humans who feel no remorse for their crimes much as we view snakes?

Our noble side wants us to do better, which is why we should recognize the pitiful fear the snake feels, unless he bites us without warning, which he might do when we have the friendliest of intentions. We have to draw the line somewhere and hope that our contrition and the gods' forgiveness for our smiting the snake will somehow make everything right in the end.

ON MATH

LIKE CALVIN OF comic book fame, I am a math atheist. Starting in the third grade, I ran into some procedure nearly every year which knocked me down and kicked me. Carrying gave me fits. I survived common arithmetic fairly well and am amazed at how good I am today at it compared to the calculator cripples we are producing.

Algebra was my downfall. Had it happened to me today, I would have been sure it was an Al Queda plot. It made no sense to me and still doesn't. Every math course and most science courses which followed used algebra, and my math and science career died at the tender age of 14. On standardized tests, my math scores were always the lowest, 80th percentile or so. I developed a complex, which might provide psychiatrists with a field day. Furthermore, I suffer from the ethno-biological condition of Scottish stubbornness.

Now, it would be easy to attribute my math handicap to my perverse nature, but I discovered over the ages that I'm not the only one who has it. We algebra-challenged people often did better in geometry, while those who managed algebra frequently struggled with real shapes like triangles, squares and circles. Any reasonable profession would have recognized that there was a real issue here. The math and science profession blindly refused to see it.

I loved it when an uncle of mine once declared that algebra made people more logical. He commonly failed to see his own narrow-mindedness. I have observed this phenomenon in others. I remember the time my physics teacher called me in to ask why I was making Ds when my junior-year, statewide test score was fifth in a class of 250. I could only stare at him and quiver a little, though I knew algebra was the culprit. I actually liked physics because it explained how things work in the physical world.

Luckily, I went to a progressive university which required no math courses of people who did not need them, proving that everyone who told me I would have to take algebra in college was a liar. I was particularly lucky because this was the 1960s when there was a draft board lurking out there, just waiting for guys who dropped out of college. That is how serious this matter could be—a matter of life and death.

Fast forward 40 years. I teach in a school with the words, *math* and *science,* in its title. My students take part in science fairs, researching social issues based on statistics. I regularly give assignments using numbers. In fact, I once designed an independent study course in U.S. History based on numbers for a history-challenged student. She passed with an A.

I am disturbed by how much kids struggle with simple arithmetic when they are studying advanced integrated math in 7th and 8th grade. I am also disturbed when older kids cannot tell me what the complex formula (which is Greek to me) left on my board means. Small wonder they have trouble analyzing social issues.

Of what value is math to the whole population, the vast majority of whom will never be engineers, physicists, doctors, chemists or architects? All will be citizens and should be capable of logical thinking. The purpose of schools is not to provide jobs for teachers nor a market for textbooks, but the system sometimes suffers from cases of both practices. In terms of math education, it seems guilty, also, of a sadistic desire to punish those, who through no fault of their own, cannot grasp the concepts.

I've known enough math teachers to know another little secret of the profession: they do not need as much time in the classroom as other disciplines do to teach what they must teach. Consider that basic arithmetic does not grow—it has been the same for centuries—but history, the sciences and literature get bigger by the year.

What would a truly logical approach be to math education? I hear the French have one. *Vive la France!* Let us start by insisting that all students master common arithmetic, sans calculators, in grades one through eight. This mastery should include a solid understanding of percentages, ratios, fractions and all forms of graphing. There should be an accompanying emphasis on narrative analysis of what these mean when applied to practical, everyday life situations. This is nothing more than a person being functionally numerate in those things everyday life requires.

Numeracy means having a realistic sense of proportion, of knowing larger and smaller, more or less, of questioning well, of knowing that a one-point victory in the Super Bowl does not constitute true superiority. I think some portion of societal inability to understand life stems from innumeracy. A person should know that a car priced at $9,995 is costing him $10,000—not $9,000 dollars. A person should know that 50.1% of the vote does not constitute a clear majority nor a mandate.

What next? Several things must change in terms of attitudes held by colleges and universities. They, after all, are supposed to be educational leaders. They should help guide us in a new direction. In the 9th and 10th grades, students should be allowed to explore experimental, non-graded higher math. Develop, with the help of psychology, better testing for ability. Do not label kids negatively when they show genuine distress over the arcane mechanisms of algebra or geometry. In those two years, channel the math-gifted where they need to go and don't bring the precocious into the equation. The eight-year-old prodigy who can do college trig should not be allowed to drive the system nor be excused from societal development because he/she happens to be a math genius.

By 11th grade, we should know where a student belongs. If it is not in calculus or trigonometry, then put that person in a good logic course for a year. Require all students to apply arithmetic skills to social science all four years of high school. I, the math atheist, say so. With a little effort we could integrate math into several disciplines. It seems like an idea whose time has come—almost as simple as 1 + 1 = 2.

ON ONEROUS RESPONSIBILITY

As I DROVE south today alone, I found myself thinking about responsibility. It is the essence of adulthood, and it is a pain in the behind. We humans take a certain pride in accepting it, and we crave adulthood; well, we crave the more irresponsible aspects of it—fast cars, hot sex and cold beer. When the actual consequences of adult responsibility come down, it is not such a desirable thing after all.

Men are particularly put in a hard place by it, hard in the sense that men enjoy being savage 12-year-olds, and responsibility ruins that status. Having to work, having to care for others, having to be careful with money just takes the fun out of life. No wonder men die earlier than women. They are tired, worn out and dispirited early on.

Certain psychologists have argued that we only become whole, fulfilled beings when we accept responsibility for others as well as for ourselves. Now, I think this is where many of us have a problem. Taking responsibility for myself is one thing, and a hard-enough thing at that. Actually, I like having parents, or a wife, or Uncle Sam taking care of a lot of the crazy details of life—details like insurance, paying bills, medical care, savings and such.

Why should I have to be responsible for others? That is what I have hated about teaching—the irresponsibility of students, parents and administrators. I am willing to do my job. I expect others to do theirs, and when they don't, I'm upset. I take no pleasure in making them do theirs.

This leads us to the issue of being parents. Humans were not designed by nature to assume the responsibility required of parents; hence, we fail with great regularity. I've no doubt that many behaviors by men, which are frowned upon by society, are, in fact, reactions to the stresses of responsibility. By this I mean drinking, drugs, whoring, running away and war.

What of women then? By default, they often have to assume responsibility for children. Of late, women have gained more positions of authority in various institutions. Now let us see if they handle responsibility and its stresses better.

The man or woman who glories in being responsible for others is suspect. Such people may be paternalistic, condescending, fascistic, bearing superiority complexes and often believe that they deserve whatever emoluments they can extract from those they "help" by leading them. I prefer that we kick people in the posterior to make them take care of themselves. Of course, I still want my mommy, daddy and wife to take care of me. Aren't we humans a funny crew?

On Some Important Philosophies

It takes all kinds to make a world. (universal wisdom)

Déjà vu all over again. (Yogi Berra)

It's not over 'til it's over. (Yogi Berra)

As I would not be a slave, so I would not be a master. (Abraham Lincoln)

Forgive us our trespasses, as we forgive those who trespass against us. (Lord's Prayer)

Don't criticize a man until you have walked a mile in his shoes. (American Indian saying)

All we have to fear is fear itself. (Franklin D. Roosevelt)

If there were an all-powerful God, he would make all good and no bad. (Mark Twain)

Everyone is a moon and has a dark side, which he never shows. (Mark Twain)

History is not history unless it is the truth. (Abraham Lincoln)

Nothing should ever be implied as law which leads to unjust or absurd consequences. (Abraham Lincoln)

A tendency to melancholy, let it be observed, is a misfortune, not a fault. (Abraham Lincoln)

It is curious that physical courage should be so common in the world and moral courage so rare. (Mark Twain)

Mankind is more disposed to suffer, while evils are sufferable, than to right themselves by abolishing the forms to which they are accustomed. (Thomas Jefferson)

Dichos de Kermit

There is more than one way to skin a cat—schools should teach cat-skinning 101.

Where politicians gather, there is the smell of sulfur.

Denial runs deep, wide and very murky among humans.

There are many strange people running around loose out there. Be careful.

The gods, like naughty children, play dirty tricks on us.

Islam covers all but a woman's eyes, for good reason.

The best defense is a good defense. (Football coaches and fans take note.)

We all suffer the human condition.

Life is a great mystery.

Lordy, life just rumbles on.

Ignorance is the enemy.

Why?

God only knows, and he/she/it may not be too sure.

It is against everyone's religion to starve.

On Pleasure

PLEASURE AND PAIN, yin and yang. Did the gods create these just so humans could be controlled like so many lab rats? Must both affect us simply in order that both can have meaning? Both can crush and destroy people.

What pleases some, bores others. Simple pleasure does nothing for those needing high excitement. Then there are those who deny pleasure and embrace pain, and those who seem to confuse the two. The latter find pleasure in some form of pain. No size fits all here.

The mere absence of pleasure does not necessarily mean pain fills the void in a well-defined way, but the absence may well mean the presence of a dull ache, which is the absence itself—that state we speak of as feeling empty. We, conversely, speak of feeling filled with joy. I suppose it is the effort to attain a constant state of joy that often leads individuals to pursue monastic lives of asceticism and denial of life's pleasures, hoping that pure spirit will do the job. I have serious doubts that this works for most of us—or was meant to. I understand the beauty of simple pleasure, but it is still pleasure, and it can be most joyful.

Maybe it all comes back to the question about buying happiness. Happiness and pleasure are not always the same thing. While being happy is pleasant, one might be happy without experiencing any sensual pleasure. There are obviously behaviors which give people pleasure, which also create unhappiness for them and others as a consequence. The behavior of the super-rich is instructive: they become quickly bored, as do non-rich people, but having lots of money, they buy new toys, which quickly bore them. The less-rich often go bankrupt buying new toys. Boredom is the culprit. It does not please us to be bored. This is why variety is the spice of life. The most sumptuous of anything gets boring. Too much of a good thing is not a good thing.

It is possible to derive pleasure across a long span of time from the same simple things if one spreads them out in smaller doses with a strong sprinkling of diversity. Fads do not serve this purpose, nor does dogma. The principle of "to each his own" is also important. We are individually wired in such a way that each of us finds different pleasures.

In relationships, this matter of individual difference can be a problem. Absolute compatibility of pleasure and pain is an unrealistic hope. The degree of shared pleasure combined with a willingness to allow the partner his or her freedom determines the viability of the relationship. It is difficult for us to understand why others do not perceive the world as we do. I finally came to realize that our biochemical neuro-wiring accounts for most of this. For example, I dislike the smell of plastic modeling glue, even though I have worked with it for most of my life. My spouse says it smells ok. Some people sniff it. In another realm, I cannot hear certain elements of music, which excite people related to me. Apply this idea to all the senses, and one sees what an amazingly complex world we live in—and it does take all kinds to make a world.

On History's Role in Explaining the Origin of Life

I HAVE JUST finished a book about why the earth exists. The only rational conclusion is that it is all a great mystery, in spite of the efforts of philosophers, theologians and scientists to prove otherwise. The author never deals with the role that historians play in the effort, nor does he do much with dreams.

So, it occurs to me that each of us is analogous to the creation. In fact, we procreate. Why we do it is a mystery. I think it is because we are entertainment for the gods, but never mind. We do it, and so do birds, bees and educated fleas. We have no memory of our birth or infancy and little of our early youth. Perhaps those that we do have are Plato's cave shadows. They are generally fuzzy; hence, they are full of mythology. For most of us in Western culture, there is a very un-uniform written record called *history*. I used to have my 7th grade students prove to me that they existed by way of such records. They did not take kindly to the request at first, and then they caught on. Otherwise, they were a figment of my imagination.

History is rarely perfect. It always contains elements of myth and legend. Today, Americans at least love to study their genealogy. Scrapbooks and yearbooks ought to be part of this, but often are not.

The latter types of records help assure us that our more dream-like memories are real. They are often, in fact, not real. The older we get, the more much of our life seems like a dream. Sometimes they are bad ones—that is what PTSD is about. Maybe this is why humans cling so tenaciously to myth, legend, and ridiculous superstition. Many people lack solid, pleasing histories—they need a foundation in order to feel secure. They ask, "Who am I?" I am my history. God forbid it should turn out to be different than I have thought it was.

Dreams are frequently disturbing, whether scary and dark or not. They are filled with unknown people and scenes and border on insanity. We need history to know who we are, even if our image of ourselves is not wholly true. We repeat half-truths and untruths until they are believed as The Truth. The "everybody knows" syndrome takes over. I would argue that false "truth" is a form of mental instability.

The camera has played a very important role in all of this business, not that the fearful don't immediately tell you about how photos can be doctored. Through it we are allowed to go back to look at how we really were, visually speaking. This is a major step in the evolution of history—or maybe not. Now, every Tom, Dick and Harriet has an iPhone camera, but no training in how to use it well. Using them well has a lot to do with preserving history. Even our ancestors lacked that training. How many old family scrapbooks do I preserve which have nothing written in them?

Philosophy and science explain why things happen, kinda sorta. Religion has childishly simple answers. History purports to have the answers, but really holds only a part of the story. Humans look for the easy explanations, especially for why we suffer, which too often leads to scapegoating.

And we change, like it or not. We are constantly being redefined at an ever-faster pace, which makes knowing ourselves that much harder. We dwell on "the good old days," which were rarely that good. Of course, we focus on the positive aspects of them and ignore the rest— or we romanticize them clear out of reality. Even I have had to be dragged screaming and kicking into the age of computers and digital cameras. I just bought the latter today.

An interesting example of this latter phenomenon showed up in this morning's paper. Indian Market is coming, and it will include fashion design, filmmaking and all manner of nontraditional Indian arts. No doubt each Indian tribe's history is important to them, but they are redefining themselves, too, if slowly— just as we all must.

The Great Mystery flows on.

On Politics

WHAT IS A good politician? An oxymoron? Politics is the art of the possible, it has been said. I translate that to mean that politics is the art of maneuvering diverse groups of people toward common goals. A good politician is one who achieves goals which are good for the common or greater good. This is no easy task. We speak of the people as though they were homogeneous. They are anything but. Society is comprised of a complex chemistry of diverse, often competing interest groups. Each individual adheres to a variety of interests, major and minor. No group is immune to fragmentation and factionalism.

The first rule of politics is that the politician is damned if he does and damned if he doesn't. So, he spends a lot of time and energy on math, adding up votes. The individual does—or doesn't—count statistically and will inevitably feel deceived. The politician has to be vague at times, risking the impression that he made promises when he did not. People hear what they want to hear, so he often tells them that which they want to hear. Since the news travels, the word gets out that he is changing his story according to locale. Whose fault is this? The only really honest politicians in a diverse society are those who can't get elected. Honesty means failure.

There is a theory, too, that the general public does not want leaders who are visibly more intelligent and educated than the norm. Again, an honest man is doomed. Good actors who know how to play good ole boys succeed, as do those bright ones who do not let their intelligence become arrogance—they have the common touch, do not talk down to others, and they listen. At least they act these parts well.

Unfortunately, on the big screen, looks have come to count more than they should. Leaders have always been idols or devils, but now the thin veneer of appearance can override other qualities. It is doubtful that Lincoln could get elected these days, except at the very lowest levels of service.

Let us raise a toast to politicians—someone has to do it, and we are lucky that there are those with egos big enough to think they can and skins thick enough to survive the slings and arrows of outraged publics. We are also fortunate that some of them are wise enough not to abuse power beyond the limits we consider to be reasonable.

There is a difference between a leader and a politician. I was listening to a group of liberals bemoan the weakness of the Democratic Party in terms of finding a viable candidate. I think one hit a major nail on the head when she said, "The Democrats are too nice." Why are they too nice? Perhaps because they try to represent a larger, more diverse group of people, all of whom can be offended, thereby costing votes. Another woman bemoaned the lack of a sense of sacrifice by union transit workers, while a third voiced dismay over a politician's support of the death penalty.

People want action and need things done, but these politically correct liberals are paralyzed, so the conservative leaders take action, winning the votes of a smaller but more homogenous public who want action. There are times when a politician must be a leader in the truest sense of the term, and the devil take the hindmost. If he is worried about popularity, he cannot lead.

There seems to be no good solution to the ugly side of politics. Churchill said that democracy is a terrible form of government, but it is better than any other form out there. Obviously, people with fascistic leanings, extremists of all shades, and serious megalomaniacal narcissists don't believe this about democracy. Politics is a game, a game of debates, which Churchill loved, of course. No debate, no politics, and we are all happy until the dictator deprives us of something we personally want.

Viva Politicians!

On a Graduation Address

GOOD MORNING, GRADUATES, guests, students, faculty and staff.

A long time ago, in a faraway place on a similar occasion, my classmates and I were asked to work for world peace, lower the national debt and end alcoholism. Our generation has not done too well in the succeeding 47 years. I will not pass those Herculean tasks on to you, nor will I tell you lies, least of all the old stock graduation day lie that you can do anything you want if you will just put your mind to it. You cannot. You can only do what your natural talents will allow if persistently, stubbornly exercised. Stubbornness is a much overlooked, underrated quality in our culture—it lacks glamour.

How long will this speech be? Answer: long enough to reach the ground! *(Lincoln said this in reference to his legs, about which he was teased. This was the only hint to the subject of the speech, and the students got it.)* You deserve to be promoted.

He was born in poverty in 1809. His mother died when he was nine, and his father was unpleasant enough that he refused to attend his funeral. He attended the equivalent of one year of school, performed hard physical labor as a child and was on his own by age 16. His girlfriend died when she was 18, leaving him almost suicidal. Strong evidence indicates that he was clinically depressed most of his life and without benefit of psychiatrists or medications. He never had an easy time with women, though he liked them very much. He served in the Black Hawk War, rejected high command and empathized with the enemy.

He lost many elections, was elected to national office only once before 1860, and was rejected quickly for sticking to his principles. He would not hunt, once got a young man acquitted for manslaughter resulting from a drunken brawl, would not drink himself and spoke compassionately to the Temperance Union about alcoholism. He lost two sons to disease and suffered an emotionally unstable wife. When he was elected in 1860, he got only 40 percent of the vote. He pardoned numerous soldiers from the death penalty yet ordered tens of thousands to their deaths in defense of three great causes. He was vilified constantly in the press, saw his armies suffer defeat after defeat, and came under attack by members of his own party for showing compassion to the rebels. When he was killed at age 56 by a hate-filled group, he was probably saved from impeachment efforts by Congress and a painful, slow death from a debilitating disease.

He was an unchurched skeptic all his life but exhibited a spirituality far beyond most of his fellow citizens. Of this gangling, unpretty, socially clumsy, poorly educated, lower-class loser, it was said at his death, "Now he belongs to the ages." There are close to 5,000 books about him and sculptures of him from Washington D.C. to South Dakota to Hawaii, from Juarez, Mexico, to Parliament Square, London.

So, as you go forth, we can ask no more of you than that you use your talents well, treat your fellow humans with compassion and dignity, and stubbornly keep trying until your legs are solidly grounded. I wish you good memories and an interesting future. Until we meet again. Thank you.

On Historic Epidemics

We went for an afternoon walk on a beautiful, sunny mid-March day, surrounded by the vast, mountain-rimmed basin we live in. It was exceptionally quiet for a weekday. Lots of bicyclists rode by and a few contrails crossed the blue sky. Spring is clearly upon us.

So is a new bug called *coronavirus*. It means crown, which may have a double meaning at this moment in history. It no doubt accounted in part for the quiet as so much is closed down. Naturally, it has affected my teacher bug. I don't want to repeat myself too much since I have written two related essays in the last year.

Several things come to mind. Plagues are as old as human history, and humans are always befuddled by them. Mass hysteria is nothing new. Certain behaviors and events tend to accompany and to cause the spread of disease. I have said before we are not oysters, so we travel, invent, make war, love food and the opposite sex and adventure in general. All of these behaviors drive epidemics in some way. Also, science is relatively young; religion is very old—as are human tendencies to see what we want to see. I would comment on five epidemics in U.S. history.

During the American Revolution, a massive smallpox epidemic struck North America, killing thousands of all races. It saved Canada from the United States when it crippled the American army of invasion, decimated Indian tribes from coast to coast, and probably also helped the Americans defeat Britain. George Washington was a smallpox survivor from an earlier plague. Vaccination had been known since 1715, and he required his Continental regular troops to be vaccinated. The colonial militias and Indians either refused to be or just didn't believe in it, so they died. The pox-laden blanket story is a canard.

In 1835-37, a worldwide cholera epidemic reached America, where it played no favorites. Some small Indian tribes along the Missouri River were destroyed because of their small numbers and their stubborn refusal to stay away from trading posts when they were told to. The new steamboats brought trade goods and germs up the river.

In 1918-19, The Great Flu swept the world, killing twice as many people as World War I did. Actually, the war contributed to the high flu death toll. Troops, animals and flu organisms were transported around the world by steamship and railroad. Today, we have flu shots, yet there are people who will not take them out of very unscientific beliefs.

We cannot ignore the tuberculosis epidemic, which killed and crippled humans by the millions across the period of industrialization, which created crowded, dirty cities around the globe. This had a large impact on New Mexico across the late 1800s/early 1900s era. In the 1920s, roughly ten percent of New Mexico's population were *lungers*—often artists—sent here to recover on the assumption that New Mexico's high, dry air and sunshine would provide a cure. The assumption was wrong: drugs eventually eliminated the disease. However, an unforeseen consequence of TB was that it solidified the role of art in New Mexico. My own father's mother died of TB in Arizona when he was only five years old. Evidently, that led part of his Kansas-born family to Santa Fe in 1922. The rest is history.

The anti-vaccination crowd won't take polio vaccinations either. This is a very old plague tied to water cleanliness, in part—always a problem in cities. While FDR was the most famous survivor of an earlier epidemic, the worst period was from the 1930s to 1952, when his March of Dimes finally brought forth a preventative. For a time, a half million humans died from polio each year and far more were crippled. Science basically solved the problem, with help from compassion and control of fear.

I will conclude with a sixth plague. It is the paranoid, irrational hysteria which seems to be with our species much of the time to some degree. It causes us to do stupid and evil things. We have wanted to think that education would cure it, and perhaps to some degree it has. However, it appears that there will always be present those who reject the education vaccination just as much as the others.

My walk in the sunny, March air gives me solace and hope. Do take your own walks, even if you ramble a bit.

ON THE SEASONS

BEING A GEOGRAPHY minor, I was fascinated by a book I read 50-some years ago titled *Mainsprings of Civilization*. Its thesis was that our culture is determined by where we live on the globe. Nearly all the great civilizations have developed in the midlatitudes of the northern hemisphere, and all the major religions have been born of those civilizations. The geography of the midlatitudes created conditions of weather and seasonal change, forcing mankind to become more creative and inventive in order to survive. As a child at Sacramento, I used to observe the movement of the sun north and south each year. I don't think I understood it until late high school. It has fascinated me ever since. Sacramento is in a canyon. In Santa Fe, we can see Mount Taylor 90 miles away. The movement of the sun carries it behind that mountain twice a year at sunset.

This movement of the sun controls the seasons. I know it is the earth's movement, but it doesn't look that way. It has, thereby, controlled our beliefs and attitudes. On one February 1st, I noticed the first ray of sun hitting a north-facing window, where in midsummer the sun comes in for six months. This observation led me to realize that Groundhog Day is, actually, the date of midwinter. Spring will come whether his shadow appears or not.

In November, we hunt, and early snows come. We are enchanted by another piece of nature's beauty. The Pueblo people call December "the quiet time." In July, they perform Green Corn Dances at about the time we enjoy fireworks.

Out of these observations, I created some years ago Hill's Midlatitude Holy Day Calendar, which follows. It is a barcode based on the fact that we color-code our holidays. It also matches a code indicating the amount of daylight and darkness by season. It moves from the growing time to harvest to the quiet time to the starving time to rebirth. I have inserted one secular holiday in it as well. Now, take out your crayons, class, and have fun.

Our holy days are clearly based on the movement of the sun. The Greco-Roman world placed the beginning of the new year at the rebirth point. Christmas was placed where it is by an early pope to attract the pagans, like the Druids, who celebrated the winter solstice.

Enjoy the sunrise and sunset wherever you are. Happy Holidays.

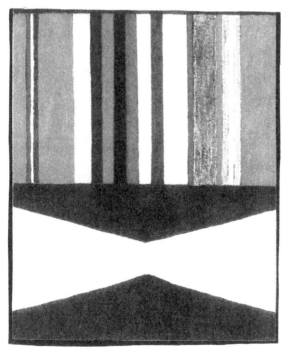

Hill's Midlatitude Holy Day Calendar

Lightning Source UK Ltd.
Milton Keynes UK
UKHW021452070620
364500UK00002B/300